"Imagine the world if each of us understood how loved and valued we are. In her book *Without Rival*, Lisa Bevere encourages us to know and understand that we are uniquely created and loved by God. Because we are, we have each been given a crucial and important role to fulfill in God's plan. This book is an invitation to pursue God and the mission he has for you."

—**Holly Wagner**, pastor and author

"We live in a culture that is filled with wandering souls looking for identity in all the wrong places. This book is a true compass that points men and women to the real source of our spiritual identity. We belong to God, he has chosen us, and we are loved uniquely. Lisa does a masterful job of bringing these timeless truths to life. This book is a must-read!"

—**Brady Boyd**, pastor of New Life Church, Colorado Springs, and author of *Addicted to Busy*

"In *Without Rival*, Lisa shares the penetrating truth about who God created us to be and how he loves each of us personally and uniquely. After reading this book, I can't imagine anyone ever doubting God's love for them!"

—**Chris Hodges**, senior pastor of Church of the Highlands and author of *Fresh Air* and *Four Cups*

"If you have ever struggled with your identity, this book will be a game changer. Understanding who we uniquely are in Christ transforms us from playing it safe to taking our place in God's great plan of redemption."

—**Sheila Walsh**, author of *God Loves Broken People* and core speaker for Women of Faith

"*Without Rival* is a truly eye-opening book that I believe will greatly impact this generation. Lisa Bevere conveys God's love in such a beautiful and vivid new way that will surely captivate every reader. As readers delve deeper and deeper into this amazing book, they will learn more and more about God's love for them as well as the importance of finding one's identity in him."

—**Matthew Barnett**, co-founder of The Dream Center

"*Without Rival* is a beautiful reminder of God's love for all people. Lisa approaches the subject with fresh revelation and expresses her thoughts in such an elegant and concise manner. This is a truly beautiful book that every reader will be inspired by."

—Caroline Barnett, co-pastor of The Dream Center

"In a world obsessed with competition and comparison, this book is a must for every mother, daughter, leader, and friend. It's time we joined hands instead of comparing what's in them. It's time for celebrating one another instead of tolerating. We are without rival, so let's make room for everyone to thrive."

—Charlotte Gambill, lead pastor of LIFE Church, Bradford, UK

"If you struggle with feelings of worthlessness or lack a sense of purpose, *Without Rival* is just what you need to silence your inner critic. God has positioned you to find contentment in the midst of any circumstance and live a life without comparison."

—Pastor Steven and Holly Furtick, Elevation Church

"Lisa will help you discover how to experience the freedom and confidence that comes from knowing you are God's exclusive masterpiece—without comparison and without rival—and that you have everything you need to reach your unique God-given destiny."

—Victoria Osteen, co-pastor of Lakewood Church, Houston, Texas

"Lisa Bevere's book *Without Rival* will wake you into new dimensions of your identity in Christ. Lisa's book is full of insight and godly wisdom. It will challenge, inspire, and equip you to pursue the Lord's unique calling on your life. If you are longing to tune in to what the Lord is speaking over your destiny, this book is for you! I highly recommend it."

—Kris Vallotton, senior associate leader of Bethel Church, Redding, California

"Lisa Bevere has been a close friend of ours for many years, and we believe the insights she shares in *Without Rival* will bring freedom to many. As you read these pages, ask God to help you overcome the desire to compare and compete, and allow him to show you how to embrace and celebrate the person he created you to be."

—James Robison, founder and president
of LIFE Outreach International

"I *love* Lisa. She is carrying such a timely word. This book is a must-read, must-believe for people. Knowing who you are and your need for others is huge! You will be strengthened as you read this, feeling the Father speak over you your true, unshakable identity."

—Jenn Johnson, worship leader/songwriter
with Bethel Music

"*Without Rival* is a brilliant wake-up call for women of all ages. Lisa's message that we are uniquely loved and called by God is so needed. I love her passion and energy that leap off of every page."

—Alli Worthington, author of *Breaking Busy: How to Find Peace and Purpose in a World of Crazy*

"Lisa's bold and Spirit-filled words will help set women free from comparison, pride, and envy. She lives what she preaches: when you belong to Jesus, you are without rival."

—Sarah Bessey, author of *Jesus Feminist*
and *Out of Sorts: Making Peace
with an Evolving Faith*

"Lisa's newest book is such a treasure. It's basically the literary equivalent of God putting his hands on both sides of our face, turning our attention toward him, and then saying slowly and firmly, 'I love *you*.'"

—Lisa Harper, author and Bible teacher

"Understanding who you belong to, your unique place in the family of God, and the character of Christ is paramount to the continual growth of a healthy heart and soul. Lisa Bevere has a unique ability to expound on biblical truth and personal revelation when it comes to these eternal principles. You will discover again not only who *you* are but who *he* is—an unrivaled, personal, and powerful Savior."

—**Brian and Bobbie Houston**, global founders
and senior pastors of Hillsong Church

"In a world where women can be marked by comparison and rivalry, Lisa Bevere does what she does best—pulls us close to her feminine heart with nurturing, empowering, and healing words: 'Daughter, you are enough, because you are uniquely loved.' *Without Rival* strips us of our need to compete, landing us safely in the heart of the Father and rooted in his embrace. A must-read for all women longing for deeper connection, identity, and purpose."

—**Christa Black Gifford**, award-winning songwriter, speaker,
and author of *God Loves Ugly* and *Heart Made Whole*

"Lisa Bevere's new book *Without Rival* is a beautiful description of the unique love that God has for each of us. The book reminds us that we have no rivals because God created us to have our unique values and identity in him. This is a must-read for all!"

—**Jentezen Franklin**, senior pastor of Free Chapel
and *New York Times* bestselling author

"My dear friend Lisa Bevere has done it again. *Without Rival* is a powerful, prophetic, and inspiring book that will help you to discover who you are and whose you are as a woman of God. Give a copy to every woman you know—I know I will."

—**Christine Caine**, founder of A21 and Propel Women

"We are not just loved equally, we are loved uniquely. In *Without Rival*, Lisa unpacks the truths that will help you recover your power and purpose."

—**Mark Batterson**, *New York Times* bestselling author
of *The Circle Maker* and lead pastor
of National Community Church

WITHOUT RIVAL

WITHOUT RIVAL

Embrace Your Identity and Purpose
in an Age of Confusion
and Comparison

LISA BEVERE

Revell

a division of Baker Publishing Group
Grand Rapids, Michigan

© 2016 by Lisa Bevere

Published by Revell
a division of Baker Publishing Group
P.O. Box 6287, Grand Rapids, MI 49516-6287
www.revellbooks.com

Printed in the United States of America

Library of Congress Cataloging-in-Publication Data
Names: Bevere, Lisa, author.
Title: Without rival : embrace your identity and purpose in an age of confusion and comparison / Lisa Bevere.
Description: Grand Rapids : Revell, 2016. | Includes bibliographical references.
Identifiers: LCCN 2016012652 | ISBN 9780800727246 (pbk.)
Subjects: LCSH: Christian women—Religious life. | Self-esteem in women—Religious aspects—Christianity. | Competition (Psychology)
Classification: LCC BV4527 .B48 2016 | DDC 248.8/43—dc23
LC record available at https://lccn.loc.gov/2016012652

Published in association with the Fedd Agency.

Italics in Scripture quotations reflect the author's emphasis.

16 17 18 19 20 21 22   7 6 5 4 3 2 1

Dearest one,

You are a daughter loved by a Father without rival, entrusted with a message and promise beyond compare, in a time without precedent. You have been chosen for this moment that is at once great and terrible. For this very reason, you must love fearlessly . . . believe outrageously . . . and hope without measure.

Contents

1

An Identity without Rival

> Our chief want is someone who will inspire us
> to be what we know we could be.
>
> Ralph Waldo Emerson

Have you ever had a rival?

I don't mean a bit of friendly competition in sports. Nor am I referring to toddlers who compete for the attention and affection of their parents.

I'm thinking in terms of a more consistent detractor. A rival certainly does not feel like a friend or like family. When rivalry comes into play, its goal is not so much to win the game as it is to remove you from the field.

But what if you discovered that the life you have always wanted was outside the realm of competition? What if you learned you did not have to lose to opt out of the game? What if you discovered you *couldn't* lose? What if you could not only think outside of the box but also choose to *live* outside of it?

Decades ago I read a book that suggested that the end of the world as we know it would be brought about by widespread alienation (rather than an alien invasion). It theorized that the time would come when the world would be divided into two opposing camps or trains of thought. When this climate of widespread division existed, then it would be a small thing to incite opposing factions into attacking one another until we experienced a full-blown apocalypse.

Any systematic division this extensive would start on a much more intimate scale. It can begin close to home where divided houses are filled with wounded people with divided hearts. There are very real forces that whisper lying innuendos that assault your mind, your will, and your emotions in the hope of causing you to turn on yourself and then to turn on others.

It is hard to escape the messages and messengers that tell us we are not good enough, young enough, smart enough, fast enough, and rich enough. We are bombarded in the hope that we will shrink to their expectations. It is only human nature that we would want to deflect this incessant bullying that implies we are never enough. When this harassment reaches a critical point, some will yield by conforming and copying, while others will rebel as they sling back accusations of their own.

We judge when we feel judged.

We shame when we feel shame.

We hate when we dislike ourselves.

When we've been bankrupted, it is not long before we want to rob others. It is a cycle in which everyone loses and nobody wins. But what if the words of Paul were true?

But godliness with contentment is great gain. (1 Tim. 6:6)

Godliness is the ability to adopt God's vantage point. This means just as we acknowledge how he sees others, we embrace how he sees us.

Contentment and being truly comfortable in your own skin won't breed complacency; they will release creativity! Turn away from all the detractors and distractions. He has his eyes on us so we can lift our eyes to him.

What then?

Rather than compete for what was never meant for you . . . you would have the energy to discover what is yours.

I pray this book brings clarity to what the unwholesome everyday muddies. Rather than striving to win a competition that gains you nothing, I want you positioned to win the war. There is a very real battle going on for the strength of your soul. It is time you took *your* place in this world. Let's expose the lies and distractions and find out who you really are.

Lost and Found

I love dogs. Recently, while I was far from home on a trip to South Korea, our beloved dog, Tia, was impounded. Apparently, a workman left the front door of our home open, and Tia left behind the warmth of our house in an attempt to brave the streets of a subzero Colorado winter. For whatever reason, she didn't find her way home that night. A yet unidentified neighbor was kind enough to take her in overnight and then drop her off the next day at the animal shelter.

Tia had a tag on, but it was next to useless because the phone number on the tag was no longer connected to our house. Then add into this mix the fact that her dog license had expired (sorry, I thought it was a onetime process) and you have a much-loved dog with a home but with no voice or identity markers to help her find it.

In Seoul, Korea, I was oblivious. My sons had wisely chosen to hide Tia's misadventure from me, but no doubt there was panic on the home front. They looked and looked but couldn't find the dog anywhere. They feared the coyotes had gotten her. As a last resort, almost on a lark, they followed someone's suggestion and called the dog pound.

When Austin arrived at the shelter and saw Tia, he wasn't sure she was our dog. The ordeal had so completely changed her demeanor that she appeared depressed rather than excited to see him. She remained in the corner of the cage, shaking and cowering. After Austin paid the equivalent of a night in a fine hotel and some hefty fines (apparently an expired license is severely frowned upon), she was ours to bring home once again.

When I returned home and learned of the whole story, I was a little hurt. Not by my sons but by my dog. Tia had been our dog for more than a decade, and this was the first time she had ever wandered away and not returned on her own. I was concerned . . . why now? Were her cataracts affecting her vision? Had her advanced age disoriented her? Was she looking for me?

Ultimately, the reason she left did not matter. She belonged to our family and her inability to find her own way home did not negate this fact. The search was made, the fine was paid, the license was renewed, and she was pulled out of her cage of shame and returned to her place on our bed at my feet. One errant night was not cause enough for us to disown her.

You probably know where I'm going with this. If we (imperfect pet owners that we so obviously are) would do this much for a dog, what would our heavenly Father do for us? Your first step in knowing your identity is found in who you are to him. First John 3:1 gives us a window into how God sees us.

What marvelous love the Father has extended to us! Just look at it—we're called children of God! That's who we really are. But that's also why the world doesn't recognize us or take us seriously, because it has no idea who he is or what he's up to. (Message)

Let's talk about just how marvelous God's love is. It is awe inspiring, spectacular, and over-the-top. It is the very opposite of mundane or ordinary. Its depth is enough to cause us to marvel. And this marvelous love is an extension, kind of like a gift with a purchase but better, because this is a gift with a gift. We were gifted salvation. God saw us in our wretched, caged state, cowering in the corner of some religious humane society, and paid the price to save us. But he didn't stop there. He drew us close, renewed our license, and identified us as his own. (All before we'd even had a bath!) You really are his. And he loves all of his children marvelously. But he loves them uniquely.

Equal or Unique?

Often in our human attempts to make all things fair, we are tempted to think that God loves us all the same. As good as this may initially sound, *same* just isn't big enough. The word *same* implies that we might be somehow replaceable or interchangeable. Like, "Oh no, I broke one of the purple glasses I bought at Target last week; I hope they still have the same ones in stock." Or using my current example, "The dog I loved for more than a decade wandered off the grid. That's okay; I'll just buy another one to replace her and I will love it just the same."

This doesn't work for me, and I don't believe it works for God either—and I will tell you why.

One afternoon I took a nap. The problem was I was on my laptop and not my bed when I fell asleep. As my head bobbed forward, I abruptly woke up to discover eight pages of the letter "t."

At which point I felt I really should go and take a real nap. So I picked up the dog at my feet and wandered off to my bedroom. As I was dozing off, I heard the Holy Spirit whisper, "I do not love my children equally."

Shocked, I sat straight up in my bed. Where did this blasphemous thought come from? I blurted out, "You have to love us the same or else it wouldn't be fair."

I don't love my children equally, I love them uniquely.

My protest was answered with, "I don't. *Equal* implies my love can be measured, and I assure you . . . it cannot. *Same* would mean my children are replaceable or interchangeable, and they are not. My heart is not divided into compartments. No one could take the place of or displace another in my heart. For you see, I don't love my children equally, I love them uniquely."

Take a deep breath and listen. *God loves us uniquely rather than equally.* Believe me, *unique* is better.

If you have more than one child, you probably already understand this. When that second, third, or later child was born, your love was not divided. It was multiplied in ways that were immeasurable. You couldn't quantify your love for each child even if you tried. How can you measure the pull on your heart? Your love for each child is unique. Each one awakens your parental love in a different manner. Interestingly, you may love something unique about one child that is the opposite trait of something you love in another. For example, I have a feisty granddaughter who is a whirlwind. She is the sister of my firstborn grandson, who is intentional and gentle. I don't compare them. I love, enjoy, and appreciate their very different approaches to life. I would not want them to act the same for the world. Neither one of them occupies more of the real estate of my heart; I love both of them completely, but uniquely.

Equal also implies God's love is measured or measurable, and it is neither. It's infinite. *Unique* carries so much more depth. There is only one like you! St. Augustine said it best: "God loves each of us as if there was only one of us."

Our Father's love cannot be likened to a pan of brownies or a cherry pie that is painstakingly cut by a loving parent into equal portions so that no child feels slighted. His marvelous love is not subject to portion control. Do you understand he loved you before there was a beginning, and his love for you knows no end? You can turn from him, run away, and make your bed in hell, but your actions will not stop his love. (Seriously, though, who'd want to sleep in hell?)

Through the prophet Jeremiah, the Lord said this about his love: "I have loved you with an everlasting love; therefore I have continued my faithfulness to you" (Jer. 31:3).

Notice the tense here. It is past. His love is a settled matter. He loved you, the real you, the unique you, with an everlasting, never-ending, it doesn't matter how old or how young, how thin or how heavy you are kind of love. He loved you when you were young and foolish. He loves me more mature and random. God is love. Our Father does not *have love* for you . . . he *is love* for you.

Our Father's marvelous love for us is infinite, intimate, and unique. And you are uniquely loved because you were uniquely created.

Unique means "the sole example of, prototype or only one," and my favorite definition, *"without equal or rival."* Our Father God stands alone without rival, so we shouldn't be surprised that in his eyes we are daughters without rival, which eliminates every reason that we should ever compete with one another.

You are the only example of you!

You are the beginning and the end of you. There is not a designer sample scheduled for mass production. In his lineage, there are no copies, or same, and no equal. There is no rival for the way you express his love to others or for how he expresses his love to you. No one can do *you* like *you!*

God uniquely created your DNA and knit your frame in secret so he could surprise the world. He authored how your heart expresses itself; he was the architect of your smile and the melody of your voice; he made all of your features with the fondest thoughts of only you in mind. He celebrated along with your parents your first smile and watched with affection your first steps.

Because of this tender, intentional care, there are multiple facets of your life that express and reflect his love uniquely.

He wove all these exceptional aspects and specific talents into the package of you, his daughter. He knew each attribute would be expressed best through your feminine form.

He knew you would represent and relate to him best as a daughter. This is the very reason he chose female for your gender. There is a very tender bond between fathers and daughters.

He didn't have another daughter in mind when he fashioned you . . . you are his delight.

This means you wouldn't do it better if you were taller, shorter, blacker, or whiter.

This also means you would not be a better carrier of the love he has entrusted to you if you were a male. God does not love sons more and daughters less. Nor does he love each gender equally. He loves male and female uniquely. Perhaps as you grew up you heard whispers, or even shouts, that your father or mother wished you'd been born a son. Maybe there was a time you wished you'd been born a male too. But know this . . . God never did.

Our Father rejoiced when you drew your first breath, and as the years unfolded, the angels of heaven rejoiced with him when you were reborn as his Spirit-quickened daughter.

Marvelously loved one, there is absolutely nothing accidental about you.

A Daughter without Rival

So what does all this mean? It means there is more than enough immeasurable, inexhaustible love for us all. You don't have to fight for your place at the table or win his love. No one can take you out or replace you . . . you have no rival.

But friends, that's exactly who we are: children of God. And that's only the beginning. Who knows how we'll end up! What we know is that when Christ is openly revealed, we'll see him—and in seeing him, become like him. All of us who look forward to his Coming stay ready, with the glistening purity of Jesus' life as a model for our own. (1 John 3:2–3 Message)

Together we're going to discover how to be our full selves—not someone else in an attempt to earn the love and acceptance of others. We're going to stop comparing ourselves with others because comparison is not inspiration. Comparison is cheating us and this earth of who we truly are. Where is the need for comparison or competition if our value and identity are ultimately tied to our innate uniqueness? We will only exhaust ourselves. You are a daughter without rival carrying a light without equal equipped to fight a battle without rival—uniquely.

So since we find ourselves fashioned into all these excellently formed and marvelously functioning parts in Christ's body, let's just go ahead and be what we were made to be, without enviously or pridefully comparing ourselves with each other, or trying to be something we aren't. (Rom. 12:5–6 Message)

This passage of Scripture reveals the two main detractors from a life without rival: pride and envy. The description of *unique*, a daughter without rival, does not mean you've arrived. What it does mean is there is a journey, and a piece of the puzzle, and a function in the body that is yours to contribute.

Pride disconnects us from the body when it whispers imaginations that exalt us beyond measure and tease us into saying, "My part is the most important part. I stand alone, self-sufficient, self-important, arrogant, and exalted."

On the other hand, *envy* tempts us to neglect our individual God-given roles in this world when it demeans our assignments. Envy says, *I don't value my role or my part, because I want you out of the way so I can have yours.*

> No one can take you out or replace you . . . you have no rival.

Both of these are two edges of a deadly sword designed to take individuals out and separate related groups of people from their function and place. Sometimes the enemy pits both ends against the middle as he attacks men in the body of Christ with rivalry and a distortion of gender pride while the women fall prey to gender envy.

Be a true friend to all of us by being an authentic you. It is time God's daughters celebrated "unique" and stopped settling for the "same" or competing for "more." You actually give others permission to disrespect you when you do not express your true self. People can always discern a counterfeit or copy from the original. Even if they don't see it, they will feel and hear it in the hollowness of your words, actions, and appearance. There is a vast difference between following an example and copying. This is one reason why you are so frustrated when you try to be someone else. Life is like a multiple-choice test, and the only wrong answers are the ones you do not choose for yourself.

We slight the designation of our Father's love when we deny our unique self-expression. And please understand that what you look like should be the least of your concerns. So many people think they express their uniqueness through their taste in clothing, hair, jewelry, and makeup. These outward expressions are accessories. They are far from the most profound revelation of who you are.

The truth is you can look different and still not understand unique.

Let's stop wasting our time looking around and allowing constantly changing public opinion to imprint its copycat image or ideas on us. Let's confidently embrace all that God created us to uniquely reflect.

Whom Do You Belong To?

I don't need to know who it is you hang around with. I don't need the name of your parents, school, or employer. I want to know the name of the one who gave his life to purchase you. And yet you are missing out on so much if you imagine the reach of his sacrifice stops there. When he found you, he didn't brush you off and put you back where you were before. He raised you. And graced you with his righteousness.

Say it now, even if it is but a whisper of your heart: *I am his and he is mine.*

Your eternal Father is the only one who has the right to define you. Your mother conceived, carried, and cared for you, but your heavenly Father conceptualized, created, and spoke you into existence. When you were lost, he redeemed you so he could once again call you his own. The day will come when time as we know it ends; then he will regenerate each of us, and we will realize this earth life was but a seed, and there in heaven we will blossom into our truest form.

I don't know where life has placed you right now, but please understand that locations, seasons, and circumstances are constantly changing. What really matters in the midst of all the ebb and flow is who you are and to whom you belong.

At the beginning of this chapter I placed a favorite quote of mine by Ralph Waldo Emerson: "Our chief want is someone who will inspire us to be what we know we could be." God is that someone. Everything he is and everything he does inspires. The Creator masterfully crafted all that we see, hear, and know as creation to reconnect us with our divine identity. He sent his Son to reestablish our relationship with him.

With this great reconnection to our true identity in place, far too many are content to allow the shallow confines of *what they do* or *what they have* or even *who they love* to define them. But it is foolish to tie your identity to something that could be so easily taken away from you. Jobs change and skills can be lost and things can be stolen. Even important relationships can be stripped from us. What you have and what you do and who surrounds you can change, but it is vitally important that you never lose who you are and the Creator to whom you belong.

If you only know where you are going, you run the risk of losing yourself along the way. If you only know what you are called to do, you may compromise yourself to achieve your goal.

And thus the age-old question, "What will it profit a man if he gains the whole world and forfeits his soul?" (Matt. 16:26).

Knowing *who you are* is vastly more important than knowing where you are going or even what you can do. Because he is your Creator, God has quite a bit to say to you about who you are. And who you truly are carries within it the revelation of what you could be.

Who Are You?

You don't have to look at what you've done or even what you've been through. Don't describe yourself by what you do. You won't need to reference your relational status—single, divorced, married, or dating. This isn't a Facebook status update. This isn't for me or even for them.

I want *you* to know who you are.

Before we go any further, pick up a pen, close your eyes, and ask your Creator to whisper his unique designations over you. Don't be afraid that you are making up words of love and value. These words are really how he sees you. Be still a moment and know. I challenge you to write down three words or phrases that he whispers over you. When you have finished this exercise, look at the words you heard when you were able to push aside everyone else's definitions of you and hear what God was whispering over your life. Are you even a little surprised with your list? Has it been awhile since you considered this perspective on yourself?

I want to assure you that God will never speak something that is contrary to his Word. *The Holy Spirit animates what God's Word outlines.* But because we have a Bible in our possession, should we only read and cease to listen? The Message translation of Hebrews 12:28 assures us that "God is not an indifferent bystander." I believe the ethereal question raised seven times in the book of Revelation remains an invitation to us today:

Are your ears awake? Listen. Listen to the Wind Words, the Spirit blowing through the churches. (Rev. 2:7, 11, 17, 29; 3:6, 13, 22 Message)

The fact that this question is repeated *seven times* in the span of one book of the Bible cannot help but underscore its prominence . . . and makes me realize I can be awake while my ears remain asleep. It is my very urgent hope that this book awakens your ears to hear.

We can yet turn and hear the voice of God. What might happen if we invite the Holy Spirit to speak into the very places of our lives that we have declared him silent? Will you let him speak to you one-on-one? Is God allowed to speak specifically into your friendships, marriage, and family? In so many ways it is our habit to turn a deaf ear to the warnings of God, and in the process we miss out on other things he longs to impart. Hearing corporately as a body begins with individuals who decide to listen. Do we dare awaken our ears to hear?

We cannot afford to doubt our God-assigned, unique destiny. If we do, we will undermine with hesitancy, fear, or anger all that has been entrusted to us. God wants to redeem, restore, and change your identity so that there is no incident, season, or name from your past left to define you. Yes, seasons, criticisms, and events can refine you—they have the potential to shape the mettle of your life, but they are not the substance of your life . . . God is.

You were sincerely sought because you are uniquely loved and are a unique expression of God's love to others. All that this identity as children of God means is just beginning to be expressed as each of his children becomes who he created them to be. In a world in which everyone is trying to discover or remake themselves, he is finishing what he authored. This book is an invitation to pursue him . . . that he might reveal you!

Discussion Questions

1. Why is knowing who you *are* more important than even knowing *where* you are going?
2. Discuss why unique is better than equal or same.
3. What are a few of the rivals that have detracted from your ability to embrace your identity and receive God's love?
4. Do you find it difficult to describe yourself outside of what you do? If so, why?
5. What does God whisper over you?

2

Our Unrivaled God

The words printed here are concepts. You must go through the experiences.

St. Augustine

Nobody like Him

In the late 1980s, the landscape of Christian worship music began to change as Integrity Music searched the globe to introduce the worship music of different continents to us here in North America. Our family would wait excitedly each month for our latest subscription cassette tape to arrive (yes, I am that old) and then play the heck out of it. Our favorite choices were rewound so many times that by the time my traveling husband listened to them, the carefully engineered highs and lows of the music were almost nonexistent. One tape in particular was a family favorite: *Rejoice Africa*. I can still see my second son, Austin, in his Mickey

Mouse underwear riding his spring-bound horse, golden mullet bouncing as he belted out the lyrics.

On one of the songs, the South African praise and worship leader passionately interjected the phrase, "Nobody like him!"

Without an ounce of hesitation, my three-year-old son did his best to mimic the worship leader's passionate declaration each time the song was replayed.

One day Austin approached me with the question I should have seen coming.

"Mom, why doesn't anyone like God?"

I did my best to explain that it wasn't that *nobody liked* God; it was that there is *nobody like* him.

God alone does not mean we serve a God who is lonely or bored. Just as the phrase "there is no one beside him" doesn't mean that no one wants to sit with him.

Our God is not passively watching and waiting. He has seen to everything and is now resting in his finished work, rejoicing when his children ask him to unpack the story.

Nor is the High and Holy One on the outside looking in.

His vantage of past, present, and future is somehow synchronized so that he sees the end in the beginning and begins things once he has ended it.

Through us he wants to be on the inside looking out, not because he needs our eyes but because we need his vision.

The God Most High describes a God above all that we could even comprehend as height. The psalmist overflowed with the awe of this revelation in Psalm 96.

> Oh sing to the LORD a new song;
> sing to the LORD, all the earth!

Sing to the LORD, bless his name;
    tell of his salvation from day to day.
Declare his glory among the nations,
    his marvelous works among all the peoples!
For great is the LORD, and greatly to be praised;
    he is to be feared above all gods.
For all the gods of the peoples are worthless idols,
    but the LORD made the heavens.
Splendor and majesty are before him;
    strength and beauty are in his sanctuary.
Ascribe to the LORD, O families of the peoples,
    ascribe to the LORD glory and strength!
Ascribe to the LORD the glory due his name;
    bring an offering, and come into his courts!
Worship the LORD in the splendor of holiness;
    tremble before him, all the earth! (vv. 1–9)

Repeatedly, Scripture poses one form or another of this question, "Who is like the Most High?"

This is not a rhetorical query merely posed for our musing. It is a life-defining inquiry that begs a resounding answer: "No one!" Our response to this declaration of his preeminence positions us to receive or unwittingly reject what God has for us. You see, there once was one who imagined he was like the Most High. It was an angelic prince who in many ways was the pinnacle of perfection. We know him as Satan, but then his name was Lucifer, the star of the morning and the archangel who covered worship. As such, he beheld God's glory and stood in his holy presence in the throne room. Ezekiel 28:12–17 describes him like this:

You were the signet of perfection,
    full of wisdom and perfect in beauty.

You were in Eden, the garden of God;
> every precious stone was your covering . . .
> and crafted in gold were your settings
> and your engravings.

On the day that you were created
> they were prepared.

You were an anointed guardian cherub.
> I placed you; you were on the holy mountain of
> God;
> in the midst of the stones of fire you walked.

You were blameless in your ways
> from the day you were created,
> till unrighteousness was found in you.

In the abundance of your trade
> you were filled with violence in your midst, and
> you sinned;
> so I cast you as a profane thing from the mountain
> of God,
> and I destroyed you, O guardian cherub,
> from the midst of the stones of fire.

Your heart was proud because of your beauty;
> you corrupted your wisdom for the sake of your
> splendor.

God fashioned him in splendor, full of wisdom and perfect in form and function. At some point, his worship must have turned to a lesser form. Perhaps it was downgraded to admiration. The path of his transgression is unclear, but we know this magnificent and wise creation began to view the Creator as a rival. In the dynamic of worship, there is an understanding that outside of God you are nothing. Isaiah describes his fall this way:

How you are fallen from heaven,
 O Day Star, son of Dawn!
How you are cut down to the ground,
 you who laid the nations low!
You said in your heart,
 "I will ascend to heaven;
above the stars of God
 I will set my throne on high;
I will sit on the mount of assembly
 in the far reaches of the north;
I will ascend above the heights of the clouds;
 I will make myself like the Most High."
  (Isa. 14:12–14)

He could not *make himself* like the Most High . . . he could only *unmake himself*, and Lucifer the morning star became Satan the deceiver. This undoing began in his heart. He began in perfection and ended up flawed. We are flawed and imperfect from our birth, and in Christ we are made whole and perfect through rebirth. Pride encourages the worship of self, while humility dethrones the selfishness of pride. When Isaiah saw the Lord, he was undone.

Then I said, "Woe is me! for I am undone; because I am a man of unclean lips, and I dwell in the midst of a people of unclean lips: for mine eyes have seen the King, the Lord of hosts." (Isa. 6:5 KJV)

This undoing prompted God's provision, and one of the stones of fire Lucifer had walked among was brought to the humbled Isaiah.

Then one of the seraphim flew to me, having in his hand a burning coal that he had taken with tongs from the altar. And he touched my mouth and said: "Behold, this has touched your lips; your guilt is taken away, and your sin atoned for." (Isa. 6:6–7)

As we seek him, we find him. With this revelation we worship and declare he alone is holy, he alone is good, he alone is the way, the truth, and the life. He alone is the Most High God.

The very existence of our God is unprecedented; he is without precedent or prior reference point. There was none before him. Our God did not evolve. Our God was and is and is to come. Just as we have learned that we are unique, our God originated unique.

Before him there were no gods, which is why we should have no gods before him. Even though our God is invisible, his existence is undeniable. The book of Romans asserts:

> But the basic reality of God is plain enough. Open your eyes and there it is! By taking a long and thoughtful look at what God has created, people have always been able to see what their eyes as such can't see: eternal power, for instance, and the mystery of his divine being. So nobody has a good excuse. (1:19–20 Message)

The English Standard Version reads this way:

> For what can be known about God is plain to them, because God has shown it to them. For his invisible attributes, namely, his eternal power and divine nature, have been clearly perceived, ever since the creation of the world, in the things that have been made. So they are without excuse.

All of creation affirms the reality of its Creator, but a definition of our God is quite another thing. It is my hope that this chapter awakens your spirit to more of your divine connection with him.

We have established that we are daughters without rival because our heavenly Father loves us without rival. To connect on a deeper level with your God-given identity, it is imperative that you really understand more of what is involved in this divine endowment. Let's expand our understanding of who our God without rival is. *Merriam-Webster's* defines God as "the Being perfect in power, wisdom, and goodness who is worshipped as creator and ruler of the universe."

You may think this definition is all-inclusive and definitive, but this is but the *beginning*. Between the very real challenge of our earthbound language and the struggle of our terrestrial vantage point, we cannot help but be limited in our interpretation of the Unlimited One. How could we possibly find words to describe the one whose very revelation would leave us speechless?

God transcends definition.

To define something, you must capture its essence with words that embody your subject. By superseding our very language, our God defies these parameters.

Okay. Forget the definition. What about a description? Again, impossible. How can we bring clarity to the vague outline when we've been blinded by unapproachable light?

> He'll show up right on time, his arrival guaranteed by the *Blessed and Undisputed Ruler, High King, High God.* He's the only one death can't touch, his light so bright no one can get close. He's never been seen by human eyes—*human eyes can't take him in!* Honor to him, and eternal rule! Oh, yes. (1 Tim. 6:15–16 Message)

If our eyesight cannot even process the appearance of our God, then how could we do more than assemble a stick figure of his wonder? Our words will fail us and we will echo the words of Job after God shows up in a whirlwind of marvel: "I had heard of you by the hearing of the ear, but now my eye sees you; therefore I despise myself, and repent in dust and ashes" (Job 42:5–6).

I truly love the way The Message unpacks these verses.

> I admit I once lived by rumors of you; now I have it all first-hand—from my own eyes and ears! I'm sorry—forgive me. I'll never do that again, I promise! I'll never again live on crusts of hearsay, crumbs of rumor.

This revelation of God awakened a hunger for more in Job. Far too many of us are satisfied with a revelation of God that is best described as "crusts and crumbs." We are content to listen to sermons, tune in to podcasts, issue "likes" on Facebook and Instagram posts, and retweet the leftovers of another person's banquet. There is nothing wrong with any of these, but in comparison to the feast God has for you, they are but crusts and crumbs. The truth is that God wants you to feed on his faithfulness. I want to whet your appetite, because there is a vast difference between talking *about* God and listening to a God who talks *to* you.

I know there are those who say we serve a God who no longer speaks. But this reasoning insults his very nature. Even if he chose to be silent, the spectacle of creation would become his voice. He sent his Holy Spirit to comfort and counsel us. As we read the Bible, it is God's Holy Spirit who instructs and leads us into all truth. God is not a deaf and dumb idol. God is not a Father who listens without a response. If we don't embrace the mystery of who God is, we won't know how to approach him. Some of the ways God speaks are through his Word, his creation, his servants, in visions and dreams, and through related members of his body. I have prayed and believe he will speak to you through the pages of this book. God is ever speaking. The question is, are we listening for him or limiting him? It is essential that we embrace this God of incomparable, limitless wonder and believe that he wants to communicate with us personally.

The brilliant theologian Thomas Aquinas spent most of his life writing about God. Both a priest and a philosopher, he labored to pair the findings of science with his understanding of our Creator. Three months before his death, however, Aquinas had a vision of the eternal realm, and the awe of it caused him to scribe these final words then lay aside his pen. Aquinas declared:

> The end of my labors has come. All that I have written appears to be as so much straw after the things that have been revealed to me.

And yet this is the very man who had carefully studied and written volumes of words that declared the glory of God and the wonder of the church. He also lived in a very different age than ours, one when words carried a greater depth of meaning and thus were chosen with great care. The opportunity to read and write was a privilege reserved for the rich, royal, or consecrated. Thomas Aquinas was a highly skilled wordsmith, yet he chose the word *straw* to describe his life's work. Straw is frequently used to describe that which is worthless. Straw is the by-product of useful grains, most often used as bedding for livestock and mulch for plants. Essentially, he was saying that the written works of his life were best suited to be trampled underfoot by beast and man.

This was the most fitting analogy he could draw between his writing about God and the reality of God as it had been revealed to him. It is altogether possible that these two sentences spoke more than any of the pages he had labored over for more than two decades. These words were woven with humility and wonder, for Aquinas experienced what Augustine had declared over a millennia earlier: "God is best known in not knowing him."

The revelation of God begins when we acknowledge that we do not in fact yet know him. Every definition we have is classified by human context and concepts. We could liken our ability to articulate who God is to that of an infant's attempt to describe its mother when it has yet to form words. In the vast universe of life, humans inhabit but a fraction of creation. It is as though we stand on a grain of sand and endeavor to describe the vastness of the ocean and all that its depths contain.

Who Is Our God?

And yet our Father wishes that we would draw near to know him better, to experience his presence and learn his voice. Just as it is one thing to know about fire and quite another to experience its light, warmth, and burn, God invites us to know him, not just *about* him. Here are a few things we know of God with supreme certainty because this is how he introduces himself throughout the Scriptures:

I am . . . one. Deut. 6:4; Mark 12:29; Gal. 3:20; 1 Tim. 2:5; James 2:19

I am . . . the Alpha and the Omega. Rev. 1:8; 21:6; 22:13

I Am . . . Who I Am. Exod. 3:14

I am . . . from everlasting to everlasting. 1 Chron. 16:36

I am . . . the author and finisher of your faith. Heb. 12:2

I am . . . the creator of heaven and earth. Gen. 1:1

I am . . . able. Matt. 3:9

I am . . . love. 1 John 4:7–8, 16

I am . . . good. Mark 10:18; Luke 18:19; 1 Tim. 4:4

I am . . . among you in your midst. Deut. 6:15; Luke 17:21; 1 Cor. 14:25

I am . . . truth and true. John 3:33

I am . . . your healer. Exod. 15:26

I am . . . Spirit. John 4:24

I am . . . Father. John 6:46; Phil. 2:11

I am . . . glorified in the Son. John 13:31

I am . . . your witness. Rom. 1:9; Phil. 1:8; 1 Thess. 2:5

I am . . . revealed. Rom. 1:17

I am . . . for you. Rom. 8:31

I am . . . over all. Rom. 9:5; Eph. 4:6

I am . . . merciful. Deut. 4:31; Rom. 12:1

I am . . . faithful. 1 Cor. 1:9; 10:13; 2 Cor. 1:18

I am . . . wiser than men. 1 Cor. 1:25

I am . . . not the author of confusion. 1 Cor. 14:33

I am . . . the author of peace. 1 Cor. 14:33

I am . . . your sufficiency. 2 Cor. 3:5

I am . . . gracious and generous. Exod. 34; Neh. 9

I am . . . slow to anger. Joel 2:13; Nah. 1:3

I am . . . highly exalted. Phil. 2:9

I am . . . working in you. Phil. 2:13

I am . . . invisible. Col. 1:15

I am . . . the God who is coming. Col. 3:6

I am . . . the righteous judge. 2 Thess. 1:5

I am . . . Savior of all people. 1 Tim. 2:3; 4:10

I am . . . unbound. 2 Tim. 2:9

I am . . . the builder of all things. Heb. 3:4

I am . . . just. Heb. 6:10

I am . . . alive. Heb. 10:31

I am . . . a consuming fire. Deut. 6:3; Heb. 12:29

I am . . . light. 1 John 1:5

I am . . . greater than your hearts. 1 John 3:20

I am . . . the God who is, and was, and is to come. Rev. 1:18

I am . . . holy. Rev. 4:8

I am . . . almighty. Rev. 11:17

I am . . . your strength. Exod. 15:2

I am . . . your song. Exod. 15:2

I am . . . jealous. Exod. 34:14; Deut. 4:24

I am . . . not a man. Num. 23:19; Deut. 4:24

I am . . . God of gods and Lord of lords. Deut. 10:17

I am . . . great, mighty, and awesome. Deut. 10:17

I am . . . not partial. Deut. 10:17

I am . . . your praise. Deut. 10:21

I am . . . with you in battle. Deut. 20:4

I am . . . a warrior. Exod. 15:3

I am . . . your dwelling place. Deut. 33:27

I am . . . your rock and refuge. 2 Sam. 22:32–33

I am . . . God alone. Deut. 4:32, 35; 1 Kings 8:60

And this isn't even an exhaustive list! I invite you to explore each of these, but in this chapter I'd like to focus on three. The first thing I want to address is the concept of God is one.

God Is One

Hear, O Israel: The LORD our God, the LORD is one. You shall love the LORD your God with all your heart and with all your soul and with all your might. (Deut. 6:4–5)

Don't mistake this designation of "one" to mean that our God placed first in some universal god contest. The reference to "one" is not as much about assigning a numerical value to God as it is about clarifying that God is the one and the only. *One* means there is no other. There is no god number two, three, or four. He alone is worthy, for he alone is God. This correlates with what Jesus said was the greatest commandment:

And he said to him, "You shall love the Lord your God with all your heart and with all your soul and with all your mind. This is the great and first commandment." (Matt. 22:37–38)

Our love for God is to be a unified expression of heart, soul, and mind with one focus and one accord. God alone is the center of our focus and the only one worthy of our worship. God understands that we do not do well with a divided heart, and he will not tolerate any rival gods, so it is a good arrangement. This command is not because God is insecure about his position with us; it is for our protection so we will not be diverted and led astray.

This can be a confusing Scripture passage in our day and age when not many people declare themselves to be worshipers of other gods. We are more likely to bow to man-made idols rather than deities with ancient names. From the very beginning, God warned his children:

> You shall not make idols for yourselves or erect an image or pillar, and you shall not set up a figured stone in your land to bow down to it, for I am the LORD your God. (Lev. 26:1)

Most of us have not erected pillars or figures of stone in our houses or yards, but that does not mean we are not carrying idols in our hearts. *An idol is anything that you give your strength to or draw your strength from.* It is where you go to get your life. It could be what you run to as a refuge. This could range from something as mundane as food or as far reaching as your involvement with social networks. If you review the list above of who God is, then you should know he is our strength, life, and refuge. No *person, relationship, organization*, or *thing* is to have power over you, except God.

For some of us, our feelings are an idol. If we *feel* beautiful, we believe we are beautiful. If we *feel* good, we believe we are good. If we live by our feelings alone, they will lie to us and it will not be long before we are led astray.

The truth is you are beautiful because our God beautifies the meek with salvation (Ps. 149:4). You are beautiful because God makes all things beautiful in their time (Eccles. 3:11). Do not allow the foolish idols and image makers of what this world calls beauty to speak *into your life* when God has already spoken blessing *over your life*! David the worshiping warrior described the practice of idolatry this way:

> Their idols are silver and gold,
>   the work of human hands.
> They have mouths, but do not speak;
>   eyes, but do not see.
> They have ears, but do not hear;
>   noses, but do not smell.
> They have hands, but do not feel;
>   feet, but do not walk;
>   and they do not make a sound in their throat.
> *Those who make them become like them;*
>   *so do all who trust in them.* (Ps. 115:4–8)

What does this mean, "those who make them become like them"? When you elevate what is human, you become limited to what humans can create. Idols are forms without function. They hold the appearance of life without any of the power of quickening it in others. Thus, their worshipers compromise their God-given senses, losing their voices and their freedom of movement. When you worship God, you are transformed into his image from glory to glory. Because there is no one like our God, there is no greater way to bring out what is unique in you than to pursue him. You can be a student of other people but never a worshiper of man.

God Is the Alpha and the Omega

The second truth, that God is from everlasting to everlasting, is but another way of saying he is the Alpha and the Omega. Alpha and omega are the first and last letters of the Greek alphabet. When the letters are paired in this context, they represent all that is from the beginning to the end. *Alpha* means "the onset, genesis, birth, dawn of, commencement, and the threshold." When it comes to *omega*, the definition is not as clear, but it means "the end, final point, and to the extreme." Perhaps the definition of *omega* is more vague because we humans are more familiar with what *has been* than with what *shall be*. This is the very reason we need to draw near to God to hear his counsel. He alone has been to the far reaches of all that we know as time. There is none like our God. The prophet Isaiah tells us:

> Remember the former things of old; for I am God, and there is no other; I am God, and there is *none like me, declaring the end from the beginning and from ancient times things not yet done*, saying, "My counsel shall stand, and I will accomplish all my purpose." (Isa. 46:9–10)

And The Message reads:

> Remember your history, your long and rich history. *I am GOD, the only God you've had or ever will have—incomparable, irreplaceable—From the very beginning telling you what the ending will be,* All along letting you in on what is going to

happen, Assuring you, "I'm in this for the long haul, I'll do exactly what I set out to do."

God declares the end of a thing at the beginning. He declares the Omega when only the Alpha has been penned. We are invited to look back and see his faithfulness. He knows how each and every day will end when it but dawns.

> For a long time now, I've let you in on the way I work: I told you what I was going to do beforehand, then *I did it and it was done, and that's that.* (Isa. 48:3 Message)

It's finished and final. He hasn't left something undone; he isn't going to be swayed to change his mind or draw back. *Jesus was his final answer.*

> So I got a running start and began telling you what was going on before it even happened. That is why you can't say, "My god-idol did this." "My favorite god-carving commanded this." You have all this evidence confirmed by your own eyes and ears. Shouldn't you be talking about it? And that was just the beginning. I have a lot more to tell you, things you never knew existed. (Isa. 48:5–7 Message)

Our God tells us in the beginning so we won't end up trusting in people or things that are doomed to disappoint or fail us. Shouldn't we be talking about what he has done rather than what we have done? Shouldn't we be more acquainted with what the Creator predicts than with the predictions of his creations?

God goes on to say:

> This isn't a variation on the same old thing. This is new, brand-new, something you'd never guess or dream up. When

you hear this you won't be able to say, "I knew that all along."
(Isa. 48:7 Message)

There it is . . .
Our God declares the end in the beginning.
In Christ, God loved us before we loved him,
caught us before we fell,
forgave us before we asked,
clothed us in righteousness before we realized we were
    naked,
and cleansed us before we were aware of our filth.

God called those who were enemies, aliens, and strangers his very own children and friends. And wrote the story of our life before we drew our first breath.

I challenge you to see this incomparable God for who he really is and begin to imitate your Father as dearly loved, marvelous children.

God Is I Am who I Am

Next, I want to address *I Am who I Am*. Exodus 3:13–14 reads:

Then Moses said to God, "If I come to the people of Israel and say to them, 'The God of your fathers has sent me to you,' and they ask me, 'What is his name?' what shall I say to them?"

God said to Moses, "I am who I am." And he said, "Say this to the people of Israel, 'I am has sent me to you.'"

I am sure Moses must have been thinking, what kind of name is that? Imagine meeting someone and when you asked for their name they replied, "My name is I am." And when you asked for further clarity, all they merely said was, "I am who I am." You would be confused and rightly so. Think of how a conversation would go: "Hi, how are you, I am?" You would appear to be talking to them while addressing yourself. The confusion on our part echoes back to the concept of our God as one, and the only one who is all-encompassing. I am certainly not "I am who I am." We are more accurately described as "I am because he is."

God is that he is. God exists because God exists. I don't exist because I exist or even because my parents got together. Ultimately, I exist because God exists. He is the Creator of *all* living spirits.

Because he is the *I AM WHO I AM*, I can say *I am in Christ* who is the I AM. I don't think we truly understand just how powerful those five words are, because if we did, we would live with a different awareness. The world will try to tell us who God is, but ultimately he was revealed in his Son. God wants to reveal himself through his Son and in the process reveal you. One day Jesus was trying to help his disciples understand this dynamic by polling them in Matthew 16:13–18.

When Jesus arrived in the villages of Caesarea Philippi, he asked his disciples, "What are people saying about who the Son of Man is?"

They replied, "Some think he is John the Baptizer, some say Elijah, some Jeremiah or one of the other prophets."

He pressed them, "And how about you? Who do you say I am?"

Simon Peter said, "You're the Christ, the Messiah, the Son of the living God."

Jesus came back, "God bless you, Simon, son of Jonah! You didn't get that answer out of books or from teachers.

My Father in heaven, God himself, let you in on this secret of who I really am. And now I'm going to tell you who you are, *really* are. You are Peter, a rock." (Message)

Do you hear this? When we have a revelation of who Jesus *really is*, then we are in a position to hear who we *really are*. Simon was really Peter. He would not always be a fisherman led by his feelings. He would be a Spirit-led leader and a rock. I can feel Jesus's excitement as he continues in Matthew 16:18–19.

This is the rock on which I will put together my church, a church so expansive with energy that not even the gates of hell will be able to keep it out.

And that's not all. You will have complete and free access to God's kingdom, keys to open any and every door: no more barriers between heaven and earth, earth and heaven. A yes on earth is yes in heaven. A no on earth is no in heaven. (Message)

When you know who you are . . . you know what is available to you. The church's identity and access to heaven's provision are intimately tied to her revelation of Christ. When we know the Word, we pray the Word, and heaven echoes yes and amen.

What Do You Call Jesus?

Your concept of God will be reflected in you. Your God perceptions will ultimately be reflected in the life you live and the choices you make. One of the ways God is revealed in our lives is by what we call Jesus. If we call Jesus good teacher, he will instruct us. If we call him wise counselor, he will impart wisdom. Islam calls Jesus both a prophet and a healer. Separately, these titles are but rumors and crumbs. But when Jesus is called on by the name of *Christ*, Son of the *living God*, then there is a revelation of Jesus the Lord in you. The book of 1 John tells us:

> Whoever confesses that Jesus is the Son of God, God abides in him, and he in God. So we have come to know and to believe the love that God has for us. God is love, and whoever abides in love abides in God, and God abides in him. By this is love perfected with us, so that we may have confidence for the day of judgment, *because as he is so also are we in this world.* (4:15–17)

Your concept of God will be reflected in you.

Within this confession an eternal connection is made, and the gap between his redemption and our reality closes. When we speak the Word of God, the distance that separates us from truth is bridged. We are positioned to identify with God based on who he is, not who we are. This means I am who he says I am. The realization and revelation of all the promises of God that "in Christ" has positioned me for are intimately tied to what I call Jesus. Is he Lord, healer, Prince of Peace, author and finisher of my faith? Do I call Jesus *God*, or do I simply name him good teacher?

Because he is love, I am loved and I can love.
Because he is life, I am alive.
Because he is able, I am capable.
Because he is my brother, I am God's daughter.

Because he is almighty, I am mighty.

Because he is healer, I am healed.

Because he is wisdom, I am wise.

Because he is, I am.

Because of who he is, I am who he says I am.

I am fearfully and wonderfully made.

I challenge you to invite the Word of God into your life experience. To begin this process right now, let's arrest this moment with prayer.

Dear heavenly Father,

I thank you that I am all that you say about me. Forgive me for reducing your image and for the times I bowed down to idols of my own making. I refuse to worship limited images set up by human hands. Holy Spirit, reveal any area in my life where these idols yet have sway. You are love, and therefore not only am I loved, but I can also love others as you do. You are my source of life and the very reason I draw breath.

You are able to finish what you begin in my life, and you have made me capable of all that you have set before me. In Christ I am your daughter, and because my heavenly Father is almighty, I have all the might I need by your Spirit. You are my ultimate healer; I will no longer look to the world to heal the very wounds it inflicted. Because you are the source of all wisdom, I will lean into your counsel.

Forgive me for the times I allowed your expression in my life to be limited to the crusts and crumbs of others. I want to know you intimately and profoundly.

I believe that you are more than I have ever imagined, and I invite you to lead me into a life of unrivaled wonder. Because of who you are, I am who you say I am. Regardless of what I feel in this moment, I am fearfully and wonderfully made.

In the name of Jesus, amen.

Discussion Questions

1. In the past, did you compare or measure the Most High with what you've known or experienced? For example, did you think he was like your father (good or bad)? How do you see him now?

2. Are there any areas where you are living on crusts and crumbs? What about rumors?

3. What do you think Augustine meant by "God is best known in not knowing him"?

4. In what areas where God describes himself as the I Am do you need to know him more?

5. In the context of "an idol is anything that you give your strength to or draw your strength from," what are some areas in your life where you've unwittingly set up idols?

6. In God's presence, when you call him who he is, whom does he say you are?

3

A Promise without Rival

If we consider the unblushing promises of reward
. . . promised in the Gospels, it would seem that
our Lord finds our desires not too strong, but
too weak. We are half-hearted creatures, fooling
about with drink and sex and ambition when infinite joy is offered us, like an ignorant child who
wants to go on making mud pies in a slum because
he cannot imagine what is meant by the offer of
a holiday at sea. We are far too easily pleased.

C. S. Lewis

Okay . . . wow.

There is unrivaled promise on your life, and it is
also your treasure. This treasure transcends measure and spans time. This treasure comes to you in the form
of intangible potential. For some, this gift is dormant . . .
alive but asleep.

It might seem easier and initially more exciting if I were to tell you someone had just deposited a billion dollars in your bank account. But even if what was left to you was more than you could spend in a lifetime . . . it would never truly be yours. For the law of earthly treasure is that it must remain in the realm of its birth. When you die, it will be left behind. But this treasure, the one you possess, transforms as it enriches and will travel with you for eternity.

This promise I speak of is unrivaled, not only in riches but also in reach. The fruit of this promise will accompany your children long after you are gone as well as meet you in heaven. This promise can never be stolen, and yet it can be sold for something as trivial as a bowl of lentils, as Esau did (Gen. 25). It is best kept safe when hidden away, wrapped in dreams and hope. As you tend the soil of your heart, this treasure flourishes and increases. Multiplied millions have the seed of this promise in their hearts, and yet no matter how many people claim their share, this treasure is never diminished.

I speak of the blessing of the King of kings and Lord of lords. It is a treasure far too vast to be bound to or measured in paper dollars or even in silver and gold. If you were left with only the clothes on your back, the treasure would remain. These riches are not attached to anything man-made; they are eternal and can be transferred with a whispered prayer. You, my friend, are royalty as surely as any enchanted princess.

A Royal Invitation

Imagine there is a knock on your door. You run to answer it and upon opening the door you discover an ethereal agent of the king. I want you to think Cinderella style, but rather than a herald there is an angel on your doorstep. This angel is so large and radiant that you can barely see beyond him, but you are aware there is a gathering of witnesses who are waiting to catch your reaction. The divine messenger calls you by name and declares loudly that you are an heiress—a princess of the heavenly realm. There is an ocean of applause. Stunned, you answer his declaration with a question. "I am?" He nods in affirmation and places what appears to be an invitation into your hands. With trembling hands you turn the envelope over. There is no mistaking your name perfectly written in bold gold letters. You draw a deep breath and lift tear-filled eyes only to realize you are alone on your doorstep. The angel and his entourage are gone. A voice calls out from within your house.

"Who is at the door?"

You answer back with a whisper, "I am."

You are overwhelmed by the sense that everything has changed, and yet when you look around at your circumstances, nothing has. The purpose of this visit was never about a change of circumstances or location. This invitation is to an unrivaled transformation within.

You glance down. You are wearing the same clothes you were in when you opened the door, but somehow they feel lighter, as though they no longer have the power to constrict, label, or identify you. As you turn to reenter the house, your mind is clearer, and you realize that this is where you live, but it is no longer your truest home. A distant city whose founder is your God and King beckons you. You walk through the family room past the slightly confused faces of your loved ones as you head for your bedroom. In the silence and the solitude of your room, you open the envelope and carefully remove the gilded invitation.

You, beloved daughter, are now reborn as Sarah, a princess of the Most High.

As you grow in the intimate knowledge of Jesus, his grace and peace will continually multiply in your life.

This royal designation means you will have access to all that you would ever need as you pursue godliness and run the course of your life. Be assured that as you delve into the Holy Scriptures, your youth and mind will be renewed and you will become aware of all the vast treasury of the great and precious promises that have been granted to you. Each of these has been miraculously provided for you! Lovely one, in case you yet doubt, this is the best invitation you've ever received! All you need to do now is to turn your back on the world that has already turned its back on you.

I took some major liberties and personalized 2 Peter 1:2–4. But read it in the English Standard Version as well:

> May grace and peace be multiplied to you in the knowledge of God and of Jesus our Lord. His divine power has granted to us all things that pertain to life and godliness, through the knowledge of him who called us to his own glory and excellence, by which he has granted to us his precious and very great promises, so that through them you may become partakers of the divine nature, having escaped from the corruption that is in the world because of sinful desire.

If Jesus had not knocked on the door of my heart, I would be left with nothing. It would have to be miraculous for me to inherit anything! My family was not positioned to leave an inheritance to my brother and me. But what would I rather have, leftovers or legacy? I learned a long time ago that a promise from God outlasts possessions.

And how do we access these very great promises? They are ours by faith. Galatians 3:14 tells us:

> In Christ Jesus the blessing of Abraham might come to the Gentiles, so that we might receive the promised Spirit through faith.

What would I rather have, leftovers or legacy?

Meet Abram and Sarai

To learn more about these promises, let's revisit a familiar story and passage of Scripture as observers. God wrote stories into Scripture so we can learn volumes through the experiences of others. As I read I watch for the skeletal sentences of each story to come alive. I visualize the story and listen to the Holy Spirit, and in this manner I see and hear things I miss when I simply read words as they appear on the pages. I ask questions: How would I feel in their situation? What would be my greatest challenge or fear?

This practice is just one of many ways to approach the Scriptures. It is not extrabiblical; it is a way of meditating to allow the Scriptures to come alive. The patriarchs and matriarchs are our brothers and sisters in this practice. This is how I *selah*[1] . . . how I pause and ponder.

First, I want you to meet Abram. He is our father in the faith. Picture a faithful, flawed, elderly, godly man. Next, there is Sarai. She is our mother of promise. She is stunningly beautiful and likewise faithful, flawed, elderly, and godly.

At God's invitation, these two people were brave enough to leave behind all they had ever known. God promised to bless and multiply the life of a barren couple. Together, they embarked on an adventure. They were looking for what they had never seen, a nation built by God. They have been traveling for decades when we join up with them. Abram is on the threshold of his one hundredth birthday, and Sarai, his wife, is on the threshold of ninety.

They had a lot of ups and downs as they wandered the wilderness. Here is my very brief summary: They weathered the strife that came when God blessed them; this caused a separation from Lot, their nephew; Sarai was put in Pharaoh's harem; Sarai was released from the harem. As they sojourned, they won a mini war, rescued their kidnapped nephew, and tithed in faith to King Melchizedek, priest of the Most High God. They experienced some serious discouragement, and they made a bad judgment call when Sarai gave Hagar to her husband to get a baby boy, who would be named Ishmael. In her disappointment, Sarai was guilty of a fit of rage and domestic violence. I'm not thinking this husband-wife-servant triangle was fun.

Here are a few things I want to highlight so they are not missed in my brief summary of Abram and Sarai's story.

1. *They were all in.* Abram and Sarai left Ur without looking back. There was no going back. God called and they followed. Period. Genesis 12:1–2 says:

   > Now the LORD said to Abram, "Go from your country and your kindred and your father's house to the land that I will show you. And I will make of you a great

nation, and I will bless you and make your name great, so that you will be a blessing."

God was making a way for a new thing in a new way. He led them forth in faith and hope. They made mistakes, but they never looked back.

2. *They separated themselves from strife.* Abram and Sarai left Ur, but they brought Lot (not the best idea). The blessing on Abram caused increase on Lot as well. When the land could not contain both of them, their herdsmen quarreled. Rather than allow contention to grow, Abram gave Lot first choice of the land. It was better for them to part than to remain together in strife. Note: if you are traveling through life with people you shouldn't be, there are times when God might enlarge both of you until you must separate. Strife will shut down the blessing of God and the effectiveness of your life.

3. *They gave as an act of faith.* When Abram tithed to Melchizedek, he was paying it forward on the promises of God. Rather than take the spoils that would come from Sodom, he gave in faith, which gave substance to his hope.

These three things had transpired when God appeared to Abram and declared the following promise in Genesis 17:4–5:

Behold, my covenant is with you, and *you shall be the father of a multitude of nations.* No longer shall your name be called Abram, but your name shall be Abraham, for I have made you the father of a multitude of nations.

An Everlasting Covenant

When you discover you are an heir, God will change your title. When God changed Abram's name to Abraham, his life expanded. No longer would he be a man without a nation . . . he would be a father of nations. In Genesis 17, God described in detail what would be the magnitude and reach of this covenant. Abraham's life would be encompassed with words such as *generational* and *everlasting*. The very ground Abraham had walked as an outsider and stranger would one day be the inheritance of his offspring and their possession forever. Just as God was with Abram, he promised to be with Abraham's descendants. I imagine Abraham wept in the presence of God as he glimpsed the goodness of their future.

In my mind, I see Abraham prostrate before God. He then rises to his knees and lifts his tear-streaked face to the stars. His hands are outstretched as though to touch the pinpoints of brilliant light set against the blackness of the clear desert sky. He is overwhelmed with gratitude. Each word of promise resounds through the very marrow of his bones. For a moment, the veil of age falls away and Abraham is young again, every cell alive with wonder.

This new name, *Abraham*, swells his heart with joy and hope. He sees Ishmael and thinks, *All this will be yours, my son; your life will be enlarged with multiplication and a blessed and vast destiny.*

The Lord tells Abraham this covenant requires a sign. This is not a beautiful, public sign like the rainbow was for Noah; instead, it is a painful, private sign. All the males of Abraham's household are to be circumcised. This removal of flesh confirms that Abraham and his offspring are in covenant with the Most High God. Then the conversation with God takes what appears to be a major segue:

> And God said to Abraham, "*As for Sarai your wife*, you shall not call her name Sarai, but *Sarah shall be her name*. I will bless her, and moreover, I will give you a son by her. *I will bless her, and she shall become nations; kings of peoples shall come from her.*" (Gen. 17:15–16)

I can almost see Abraham's confusion. A bewildered look crinkles his upturned brow . . . Sarah? The covenant is with me and I already have a son . . . Ishmael. He is my son by Hagar. This new development drove Abraham back down on his face.

> Then Abraham fell on his face and *laughed* and said to himself, "Shall a child be born to a man who is a hundred years old? Shall Sarah, who is ninety years old, bear a child?" (Gen. 17:17)

We hear a lot about mama Sarah laughing when she heard she would have a son, but Abraham was the very first person who laughed at a promise of God. Abraham doesn't stop with laughter, however. He goes as far as to offer God an alternative:

> And Abraham said to God, "Oh that Ishmael might live before you!" (Gen. 17:18)

It sounds to me like Abraham was trying to insert Ishmael into the plan. Why go to all this trouble with Sarah? New name or not, she has an old womb and an old husband. I so understand where he was coming from. But God would have none of it and counters:

> God said, "*No, but Sarah your wife shall bear you a son*, and you shall call his name Isaac. I will establish my covenant with him as an everlasting covenant for his offspring after him." (Gen. 17:19)

"*No, but Sarah your wife* . . ." is pretty clear. It is as though God is reading his mind. Imagine that! God hears Abraham and he blesses Ishmael, but *not* as part of the everlasting covenant.

When two people become one in marriage, a covenant with God involves both of them. Of course Abraham loved Ishmael, and it was only natural that he wanted all that God had promised for him. But Ishmael was the son of a bondwoman, bound to the realm of striving and flesh. The promise without rival would have to come through a sign and wonder without precedent. A very old, barren woman would have a baby:

> But I will establish my covenant with Isaac, whom Sarah shall bear to you *at this time next year.* (Gen. 17:21)

How often do we do the same thing?

God tells us he is going to do a new and miraculous thing, and we waver in unbelief? He says he is about to enlarge our lives, and we tell him there is no need to go to all that trouble . . . *just bless what I have.* What we have and what we do are not vast enough. God wants to get involved. He is thinking generationally. The covenant would come through Isaac, the one who is yet to come. The very one Abraham laughs at . . . not the one he fathered in the flesh!

I am so encouraged by Abraham's humanity. In it is a lesson for all of us. God in his mercy will even bless what we build in our own strength, but his everlasting covenant is established beyond the realm of human provision.

New Name = New Destiny

According to Hebrew tradition, names contain the potential and destiny of the individual. Therefore, a name change has the power to change your nature, which in turn makes room for your destiny. For example, we intentionally chose the names of our sons with the hope that they would grow into the likeness of their names. I learned this from my Father God, because each time I speak their names, I am declaring the meaning of those names over their lives.

God often changed the given name of someone when that name no longer expressed their nature. The persecuting Saul was renamed Paul, and the fisherman Simon was dubbed Peter, the rock, by Jesus. Isaac's son Jacob's name was changed to Israel, which means "prince of God." Our God is in the name-change business. I sometimes think of it as a witness protection program in which we all function under the identity of the name of Jesus.

When God entered into a covenant with Abram he increased Abram's capacity by changing his name. I have a brilliant friend, Brian Bileci, who is a Messianic rabbi, and he explained the significance of these name changes. To enlarge Abram's name to Abraham, God split his name down the middle and added a letter from his very own name to Abram's. The name *Abram* means "the father is exalted." The expanded name *Abraham* means "father of a multitude."

This new name declared *who* Abraham would be. It was a name that would never be fully realized in Abraham's lifetime. Because Abram's life had exalted God, his legacy would be multiplied beyond measure. Never forget, *identity is intimately attached to your destiny*. Rabbi Brian also pointed out that God's promise did not come to pass until God expanded Abram's wife's name as well. *Sarai* means "Jehovah is prince," which was changed to *Sarah*, which means "princess of God." God added a letter from his own name, *Yahweh*, to hers.

This name change identified who Sarah was in the mix. It intimately related her to God while at the same time declaring that all her daughters of promise would likewise hold a royal position. The new name took Sarah's hand out of the matter and put God's hand in.

When Sarai's name was taken from a masculine declaration ("Jehovah is prince") to a feminine role ("princess of God"), its meaning was softened and positioned as receptive. Abraham's new name increased to include a multitude, and this seed of promise would need soil of promise as well. Sarah's very life became his soil, a womb alive with promise.

The renaming of Sarah broke up her fallow ground and prepared it for the enlargement entrusted to both Abraham and Sarah. God said of Abraham that he would be the *father of a multitude of nations* and of Sarah that *she shall become nations; kings of peoples shall come from her*. God literally added imagery and vision to both of them.

When people are honorably related to one another and to their God, God steps in to do the impossible. Barren wombs are quickened with life and strengthened to give birth, loveless marriages are healed, sons and daughters are delivered from demons, and children are raised from the dead. Hope is restored, faith is ignited, love triumphs, and the enemy is pushed back as voices of deception are silenced.

Whether you realized it or not, you experienced a name change when you were born again. Your name was enlarged as well. Jesus, the promised seed of Abraham, didn't merely change our names by enlarging them with a letter from his own. He gave us unlimited access to the Father through the use of his name. As John 16:26–27 says:

> *In that day you will ask in my name*, and I do not say to you that I will ask the Father on your behalf; for the Father himself loves you, because you have loved me and have believed that I came from God.

Jesus was stripped naked and covered with our shame when he took our place on the cross. He yielded his entire spotless life on our flawed and tainted behalf, and through his utterly complete sacrifice he saved us to the uttermost, making room for all of us, every son and every daughter of promise.

You've Got to Be Joking!

Our story continues in Genesis 18 when God visits Abraham again. Abraham is seated at the entrance of his tent, where he is shaded but still has a chance of catching any breeze. He lifts his eyes and beholds three men standing before him by the oaks of Mamre. Most scholars feel these men are angels. Abraham runs to them, bows down, and compels them to stay:

> "O Lord, if I have found favor in your sight, do not pass by your servant. Let a little water be brought, and wash your feet, and rest yourselves under the tree, while I bring a morsel

of bread, that you may refresh yourselves, and after that you may pass on—since you have come to your servant." So they said, "Do as you have said." (Gen. 18:3–5)

I love that he intercepts these travelers and detains them with honor. And Abraham definitely underpromises and overdelivers. He runs first to Sarah and instructs her to make cakes from their finest flour. Then he goes to his herd and chooses the finest calf, which he delivers to a young man to dress and prepare. When this is finished, he presents them with curds and milk. The feast he serves his guests is quite a bit more elaborate than a morsel of bread!

Abraham is with his guests when a question arises:

> "*Where is Sarah, your wife?*" the visitors asked.
>
> "She's inside the tent," Abraham replied.
>
> Then one of them said, "I will return to you about this time next year, and your wife, Sarah, will have a son!"
>
> Sarah *was listening to this conversation from the tent.* (Gen. 18:9–10 NLT)

When I read this passage, it is as though I am suddenly in the tent with Sarah. I peer through the folds and look out over her shoulder. Abraham is out in the open among his guests in the dappled shade of a tree. The sound of their voices carries easily on the dry desert breeze that ruffles their garments as it courses through the trees and tents of the oasis.

Sarah listens from the darkened confines of a tent, close enough to hear but separated from their conversation. Sarah is careful not to make a sound, but Scripture reveals her thoughts:

> Abraham and Sarah were both very old by this time, and Sarah was long past the age of having children. So *she laughed*

silently to herself and said, "How could a worn-out woman like me enjoy such pleasure, especially when my master—my husband—is also so old?" (Gen. 18:11–12 NLT)

This mirrors Abraham's reaction, which makes me wonder . . . is this the first time Sarah heard this? She is obviously caught off guard. Sometimes a promise is drawing closer when it has never seemed more impossible.

In Genesis 17:21, we heard "at this time next year . . ." and when the promise is repeated in front of Sarah, it is, "about this time next year . . ." Apparently, the timetable has shifted. There is no way to know for certain how much time has passed between Abraham's conversation with God and the appearance of these angels, but it could not have been long. A good guess would put it at less than a month. The Lord is determined that Sarah is part of this conversation.

> *Then the* Lord *said to Abraham, "Why did Sarah laugh? Why did she say, 'Can an old woman like me have a baby?' Is anything too hard for the* Lord*? I will return about this time next year, and Sarah will have a son."*
>
> Sarah was afraid, so *she denied it*, saying, "I didn't laugh."
>
> But the Lord said, "No, you did laugh." (Gen. 18:13–15 NLT)

Sarah not only laughed . . . she lied! She was scared because it was one of those *you've got to be joking* laughs . . . more of a scoff.

Where Is Sarah, Your Wife?

The verses before and after the previous passage made me wonder just how much more was implied and yet left unspoken. I emphasized some things I want to address. Some of these are issues that previously escaped my notice.

First, I want to look at the question "Where is Sarah?" Why is she hiding in her tent? Why isn't she beside her husband and part of this conversation?

I know you know the end of the story, but it is important that we remember that Sarah did not. In light of her age, she may have felt that her story was over and her life was spent. She may have felt her husband's liaison and her abusive treatment of Hagar had disqualified her.

She didn't realize the pain she had been through and the mistakes she had made in the midst of repeated disappointments and hard circumstances had worked depth into her sojourning soul. Getting pregnant doesn't require depth. Shallow and careless can land you pregnant. But Sarah was going to be the mother of Isaac and to the nation of Israel, and she needed to be ready.

For thirteen years she had watched the boy Ishmael grow up. She had hoped to raise Hagar's son as her own, but Ishmael didn't feel like her son. Abraham was content, but Sarah was broken. The odds seemed unfavorably stacked against her. But even more tragic than all of this is the realization that Sarah and Abraham seemed to have forgotten who she was.

The next thing that struck me was the question, "Where is Sarah, your wife?"

When someone visits our home and they are looking for me, they do not ask John, "Where is Lisa, your wife?" The distinction is unnecessary. This clarification would only make sense if there were more than one woman named Lisa living in our home. For example, if one of my sons married a Lisa, there would need to be clarity: "I am here to see Lisa your wife, not Lisa your daughter-in-law."

Someone who knows us would simply ask, "Where is Lisa?" If they don't know us and want to speak to the woman of the house, they would ask John, "Where is your wife?"

It intrigues me that these visitors knew *both* Abraham and Sarah and yet asked for her by both her name and her relationship to Abraham.

Could these angelic visitors have been saying, "Abraham, we are here to remind you that Sarah is your wife. I know your life together looks different in this season and that you had a child with Hagar, but Sarah is still your wife." This may explain why Sarah was content to *listen in* on a conversation she should have *joined in* on. Visitors would have been rare in her nomadic world. Abraham jumped when he saw the three men standing by the trees outside the entrance of his tent. As we read the account in the Bible, it sounds like the food was prepared in a matter of minutes, but this feast would have taken hours to prepare.

Why would any of us be content to listen in rather than jump in on a conversation about God's promises? Perhaps the visitor looked around and said, "I see the father of faith; where is the mother?"

If by some chance a contingent of angels or the Lord showed up at my house and John invited them in for lunch, John would have to force me out of our family room. To be honest, this would never be an issue at my house. John's guests are my guests and my guests are his. For argument's sake, if for some reason I was not in the room and I happened to overhear them ask about my whereabouts, I would oblige them and make an immediate entrance!

I have no reason to believe Sarah was asked to leave or even that Abraham excluded her. I find myself wondering if she removed herself from the equation. This problem arises when people are so intimately acquainted with disappointment that they forget who they are. Hope will hurt. So they hide, then they laugh, and then they lie.

Regardless of the reasons Sarah was on the outside looking in, God put Sarah back into the mix. I believe it began with a reminder to both Abraham and Sarah that she was still his wife. This declaration served to push aside her rival, Hagar, and in the process reminded everyone involved of who she was. Sarah was the princess.

Why Question Abraham?

The next issue that stood out to me in this story was the fact that Sarah was the one who laughed, but Abraham was the one who was questioned:

> Then the LORD said to Abraham, "Why did Sarah laugh? Why did she say, 'Can an old woman like me have a baby?'" (Gen. 18:13 NLT)

Why question Abraham about something Sarah did? When I see this, it really does feel as though the conversation of Genesis 17 had not been shared with Sarah. Maybe Abraham was still processing what God had shared with him. Maybe he had not wanted to tell Sarah. There are times when John and I forget to relay information to each other. Or maybe they had talked and discounted the promise. But one thing is apparent: the promise of a son for and by Sarah had not been nurtured in her life. The messengers ask Abraham:

> Is anything too hard for the LORD? I will return about this time next year, and Sarah will have a son. (v. 14 NLT)

In a year there would be a son for Sarah. I find it rather comical that Sarah lied and denied laughing when she was not even the one being questioned; Abraham was. I also find it extremely comforting that our Father, the God of the everlasting covenant, heard her silent laughter, because it assures me he hears the silence of a weeping heart.

There is a vast difference between laughing at an idea and laughing with joy. Sarah's life was void of laughter. The birth of Isaac would change all that. Abraham and Sarah had started their journey together, and they would bring forth the promise when they learned to laugh again together. Promises require that husbands and wives, brothers and sisters, and men and women have conversations. For far too long the

God needed the longing and depth of Sarah to build his covenant people.

women have hidden, but God wants you to know he wants you to be part of the conversation. God needed the longing and depth of Sarah to build his covenant people. Galatians 4:22–23 tells us:

> For it is written that Abraham had two sons, one by a slave woman and one by a free woman. But the son of the slave was born according to the flesh, while the son of the free woman was born through promise.

Who Protects Sarah?

Before Sarah held Isaac in her arms, there was yet one more conversation she chose not to be a part of. This one is an absolute mystery to me, but this time when she remained silent and lied, God stepped in:

> And Abraham said of Sarah his wife, "She is my sister." And Abimelech king of Gerar sent and took Sarah. But God came to Abimelech in a dream by night and said to him, "Behold, you are a dead man because of the woman whom you have taken, for she is a man's wife." (Gen. 20:2–3)

I am glad God spoke up on her behalf because it appears both of them were content to be silent. What were they thinking? God was doing a *new* thing, but they were still relating to each other in an *old* way. This dynamic of brother and sister was never right, but now it was more wrong than ever. There had been a name change and Sarah was on the threshold of conceiving Isaac.

Sarah was obviously a woman of unrivaled beauty . . . but she was ninety! She must have aged *extremely* well, or perhaps God had radically *renewed* her youth in preparation for Isaac. In any case, Abraham, knowing that Sarah was about to conceive and bear their child within the year, should have shielded his wife from the advances of King Abimelech. Otherwise, how could Abraham be sure that she bore *his* child? Too often we think silence is submission when it is not . . . it is lying. Submission is knowing how and when to speak. This was definitely one of those times.

At their age, Abraham and Sarah may have been living with each other as brother and sister, but those days were over. If this had not been their relationship before her name change, it certainly should have been crystal clear after the angelic visit. Sarah's and Abraham's renewed names needed to translate to a renewed intimate relationship. Both of them understood that she would be pregnant with their child in less than a year. Sarah went along with the half-truth, but you have to wonder, what were they thinking?

> Then Abimelech called Abraham and said to him, "What have you done to us? And how have I sinned against you, that you have brought on me and my kingdom a great sin? You have done to me things that ought not to be done." (Gen. 20:9)

After Abraham explained the dubious reason for his deception, King Abimelech nevertheless blessed Abraham and invited them to dwell in his land. Abraham prayed for Abimelech, and God opened the wombs of all the females in his household. It is ironic that Abraham prayed for the very thing that he had yet to see in his own life. God protected Sarah even when her husband placed his safety above hers. God spoke to a king in a dream to protect her because she was a precious treasure to him. We can trust God with our safety and believe that he will bring forth the promise on our lives even when those closest to us—even our own husbands—let us down.

Free Woman versus Slave Woman

In 1 Peter 3:6 we read, "And you are now her true daughters if you do right and let nothing terrify you [not giving way to hysterical fears or letting anxieties unnerve you]." Sarah never birthed a daughter, but this Scripture states we can be her true daughters. We are daughters of promise, the daughters of the free woman, when we don't allow fear to control our actions and do not allow worry to steal our courage.

Sarah was the free woman who esteemed and honored God and her husband. Hagar, on the other hand, was a bond-woman who despised her mistress, Sarah. Hagar's offspring, Ishmael, followed his mother's pattern and mocked Isaac. Sarah understood there had to be a separation of the bond from the free. And we must as well. In Galatians 4:30, we read, "Get rid of the slave woman and her son, for the slave woman's son will never share in the inheritance with the free woman's son" (NIV).

The slave woman's son was denied a share of the inheritance. He lost his father and all he had known as family. Both the free woman and the slave woman had the same husband. They both had sons. Yet their relationship with Abraham was very different. Hagar represented the flesh and its bondage. Sarah represented the free and the promise. Galatians 4:22–26 describes it this way:

> Abraham, remember, had two sons: one by the slave woman and one by the free woman. The son of the slave woman was born by human connivance; the son of the free woman was born by God's promise. This illustrates the very thing we are dealing with now. The two births represent two ways of being in relationship with God. One is from Mount Sinai in Arabia. It corresponds with what is now going on in Jerusalem—a slave life, producing slaves as offspring. This is the way of Hagar. In contrast to that, there is an invisible Jerusalem, a free Jerusalem, and she is our mother—this is the way of Sarah. (Message)

I love this phrase "this is the way of Sarah." An incorruptible beauty, she was a natural foreshadowing of the ageless, fadeless beauty found in Christ. You were born as the result of a promise.

Abraham, the father of faith, and his princess, Sarah, are examples that pattern Christ and his bride, the church. We are called to adapt ourselves as dependent on and secondary to Christ. He is our head, and all who believe are subject to his lordship, leadership, and authority. But we have no reason to fear. He is our maker-husband. He has forged us with his love.

Stop Hiding!

If God has placed a longing within you, then he will give you the strength to forebear and bring forth. This strength comes when God visits your life with promise. Maybe these pages are like Sarah's visitors. Maybe these words have come to remind you who you are.

The truth is that there is no substitute for hearing God speak directly to you. You need to jump in on conversations with God that concern your destiny. We need what you carry on your life. This is not the time for women to hide. It is time for us to run out at the mention of our names, yelling, "I'm here! I'm here and I want to hear!"

If you want to live a life that is unrivaled, you must stop hiding and be part of the conversation.

A lot can happen in a year. It turned out to be a year like no other for Sarah. Which is not surprising when you have a year bookended by visits from God.

Do you realize this year could be the same for you? This year could begin in the shadows with a laugh and a lie and end with you embracing a promise.

You may be thinking, wait a minute, I am not lying.

You are if you are saying any of the following:

It's too late.

I'm too young.

I'm too old.

I'm not qualified.

I've made too many mistakes.

I'm fine.

I don't need a dream.

Don't lie and say that you do not long for more. Don't deny your dreams. When you do, there is first a laugh and then a lie as the door of your heart shuts. Throw open your heart and embrace all the miraculous wonder you've been invited into. Rather than mock the invitation, that we could ever live a life that is at once both miraculous and divine, let's laugh at the ridiculous wonder of it all! We are like Cinderella, and this world could be likened to our evil stepsisters. How long will we continue to cry by the hearth filled with yesterday's ashes when the Prince is at our door? You have everything you need to live the life only he could dream for you. Why have you been content to let someone else or even the past RSVP for you?

So what are you hiding from?

What is the dream that you now mock? What is the hope? You know that nervous laughter that catches in your throat in an attempt to cover what is now too painful to be taken seriously? Listen! You are neither qualified nor disqualified. You are in on this promise because of Christ.

Or maybe your life is no longer a place of pain. The ache is gone and all that is left is numbness. Is it a place that when God touches it you cry? Far too many are empty, so they laugh in an attempt to mock hope.

Is it because on some level you are like your father Abraham when you believe that there are some things that are just too hard for God? Is it too hard for him to weave meaning into your life?

Is it too late for him to put love into your world? What is it that you think is too hard for him to do for you?

In Galatians 4:4–7, we read:

> But when the time arrived that was set by God the Father, God sent his Son, born among us of a woman, born under the conditions of the law so that he might redeem those of us who have been kidnapped by the law. Thus we have been set free to experience our rightful heritage. You can tell for sure that you are now fully adopted as his own children because God sent the Spirit of his Son into our lives crying out, "Papa! Father!" Doesn't that privilege of intimate conversation with God make it plain that you are not a slave, but a child? And if you are a child, you're also an heir, with complete access to the inheritance. (Message)

You were a kidnapped heir who has been ransomed. One of the most glorious, courageous things you will ever do is to live in the fullness of all that the death of Jesus purchases for you. You find out all that is yours by reading his Word as though it is a personal letter rather than a historical account.

Then you use your voice to affirm his Word in your heart. Whether it looks like it or feels like it, you are and have all that God's Word says about you. Even now, today, God is giving you a new name, fulfilling his promises, and affirming your place as a child of God. God's destiny for your life, and his words over you, are not limited to your current situation. His promise to you is unrivaled. Don't hide from it.

Embrace it.

Discussion Questions

1. Did you know that God has invited us to partake of his Son's divine nature *now* through the promises found in Christ?

2. Is there an area or relationship that is a constant source of strife that you might need to separate from or mend before God can bring forth his promise on your life?

3. Are you hiding? If so, from what?

4. Are you listening in on conversations that God needs you to be a part of? Why?

5. When is silence not submission?

6. Is there a promise that God has made to you that you are laughing at and lying about?

7. What steps can you take to change this dynamic of being on the outside looking in to one of active, passionate involvement?

4

Don't You Dare Compare!

Comparison is the thief of joy.

Theodore Roosevelt

*T*his chapter should probably come with a warning!
What you are about to read is raw and revealing.
The following account is a sadly true and embar-
rassingly ridiculous story about me. I hope none of you has
suffered from the temporary insanity disorder I am about to
lay down here in words, but if you have experienced this . . .
you are not alone. Here we go.

My day started out innocently enough. I shuffled into
our kitchen with my robe wrapped tightly over my flannel
pajamas to ward off yet another frigid January morning in
Colorado. John had been up for more than an hour already
and was quietly reading in his study. I puttered around the
kitchen hovering in front of my espresso machine while the
blur of my two sons prepared to head out the door for the day.

Austin was off to work and Alec was off to school. When the front door closed, I settled down on the sofa to sip my second round of a perfect compilation of espresso and whipped cream topped off with shavings of unadulterated cocoa, cinnamon, a dusting of raw sugar, and a sprinkle of cayenne. (Can I just say, I wish I could make all of my friends one of these?) The winter sun was just rising over our backyard. I curled up on the sofa to watch the pink rays chase away the deep blue shadows. Today there was no flight to catch. No early morning meeting to shower for. I could ease into my day just the way I liked: slowly. I sighed and cupped the fluted glass, savoring the warmth that traveled throughout my being as I sensed blood beginning to flow to my brain. There was perfect stillness.

Which is the very reason I should have reached for my Bible and the current devotional I was exploring or even just paused to bask in God's goodness to me.

I should have known better than to turn on my phone. Believe me . . . I know now. But one of my weaknesses is also one of my strengths. I see social media as an opportunity to connect with my friends. Flipping through posts would be kind of like having coffee with confidants. A longing for connection with others is great if it's the right time and place. This wasn't either. I am one of those who should first connect with coffee and then the Holy Spirit before I go public.

The List

As I scanned my Twitter feed, I began to recognize a thread running through the stream of my friends. People I know, love, and even feel protective of were acknowledging some-one who had included them on a list. But this was not just any list. This was THE LIST. A list I very much wanted to be part of.

Okay, at this point it is important that I lend you some context.

It is a list that is reborn and renewed each year. Over the past few decades, different organizations and individuals have been responsible for constructing "the list."

This time an individual rather than an organization had created the list. Its author was a woman . . . someone I knew of but didn't know. But the fact that we didn't know each other didn't mean that I didn't want to be on her list.

I scanned the names. Because it was alphabetized and my last name begins with a "B," it wasn't long before I realized I had not made the list . . . again.

I've never actually been on the list. But apparently this time just about everyone else I knew was on it. People I mentored had made the list. Someone who translates my books into Spanish had made the list.

You may be wondering . . . what was this list and why was it so important to me?

It was a list of the top one hundred female ministers in America.

My heart began to race. Ridiculous questions and com-parisons flew through my mind. Why wasn't I on the list?

Was it because I didn't blog enough?

My mind began to scramble . . .

Why hadn't more than a million books sold and over two decades of traveling and ministering to women earned me a place on the list?

I am a good friend. What about being married for thirty-plus years, raising four sons, and having a family that actually loves being together?

I read the postscript that trailed the list. Apparently, the woman who compiled the said list admitted that there might be room for oversight and some women who should have been added to her list . . . didn't make it. To rectify this she had provided room for additions.

I scrolled down.

Would it be wrong to add my own name?

Was I serious? Of course it would be!

Maybe I could have my assistant add my name. Realizing I was teetering ridiculously close to the brink of junior high insanity, I went looking for my husband.

I stormed into his office, a fluffy whirlwind of pajamas, bewailing, "John, I'm not on the list . . . again!"

My Bible-reading babe looked up at me over the edge of his reading glasses. He was confused. He was unfamiliar with the list. With my arms flailing about I began to explain what the list was. He didn't flinch. I shared who was on it and my obvious frustration of not being on it. He didn't move out of his chair. He set down his Bible highlighter and raised an eyebrow. When my rant was done, he calmly suggested a few Bible passages for me to review.

This was not the response I was looking for! I wanted him to say, "Lisa, I am so sorry. I agree there has been an awful mistake. Bring me my phone. I will add you to the list." But he didn't.

I countered, "I am not reading those Scriptures—I can quote them already! This is not what I need from you right now! Don't you see? I'm over fifty and I will never be on the list!"

John asked, "Who created this list?" I told him the name . . . he didn't recognize it.

"Do you know this woman?"

I shook my head. He nodded slowly and looked down again at his Bible as he repeated the recommended verses with one additional verse for good measure.

No sympathy was going to be found in the company of my husband. I stormed out of his office yelling, "I don't need to read those Bible verses to know I am wrong! I *know* I am wrong! But knowing I am wrong doesn't make this feel *right!*"

I needed a female. I stepped outside onto our deck, braving the cold of subzero temperatures in my pajamas so my husband would not hear the repeat of my rant. I did at least have the forethought to dial a truth teller rather than a sympathizer. I prefaced the story with an *I know I'm wrong* disclaimer . . . then I unpacked the whole saga of the list.

"Am I on the list?" she asked.

"Of course you are! Everyone is on the list but me!"

"Who cares?" she volunteered.

"Obviously I do, and of course you don't care, you're on it," I countered. Then I confessed, "I don't want to care, but I do. I know it's wrong and I just have to tell someone. John has already suggested Scripture passages for me to read . . ."

Silence.

Have you ever had one of those moments when you feel as though you are on the outside of yourself watching a crazy woman?

That's the moment I was having. I was sounding more ridiculous every time I spoke. I needed to quickly end the phone call I wished I had never made. I blurted out, "I am coming to you as my confessor. I want to get on the other side of this. I need to be on the other side of this!"

She agreed with me wholeheartedly (that I was wrong), and we hung up.

I knew what was right. My husband knew what was right. My friend knew what was right. But it still felt wrong.

Now I was mad at the concept of the list and frustrated with this year's author. I mean, who does such a thing? After all, when I looked at it again, I saw there were other people who should have been included on this list who had escaped her notice . . . Maybe I should make a list. I could include them on it! After all, I had more Twitter followers and Facebook friends than the author. What made her list valid? I pondered this course of action for possibly . . . ten seconds. There was no way I was going to do that!

My attempt at listing people would be limited at best, and no matter how careful I was in constructing a list I was sure to leave someone out. Did I want to incite in them the very same conflict I was currently navigating? (Except I doubted anyone I might mistakenly exclude would be as absurd as I had been for the last half hour.)

I put down my phone, closed my eyes and took a deep breath, and let it go. As I exhaled, I heard the Holy Spirit gently ask, "Lisa, would you be this upset about the list if you were on it? Would you call the list destructive and invalid if it held your name?"

Truth time. I would not have. Instead of being angry, I would have used my social media platform to thank this woman I didn't know, and I might have retweeted as a way of pointing others to the list.

I was so busted.

Yes. I am the wife of one, the mother of four, and a grand-mother, and yet when I disconnect from my true identity, I still can struggle with the cruelty of comparison. In that way, the list was a gift because it located me.

When we look to others for our affirmation, we will always feel as though we are on the outside looking in. To be quite honest, there is no single person who can completely fill the void of affirmation in your life. (Sorry—even if your husband were perfect, it is not going to happen.) There is no lifetime achievement, list, or award that can ever write with assurance the words God alone can inscribe on your heart:

Loved, beautiful, valued, intimately known . . . mine.

The Thief of Joy

No matter what it looks like from the outside, God alone understands what causes the quaking of a woman's heart, and God alone knows how to calm the frenzy of women in pajamas who forget to still their souls before comparison comes to steal their peace. I can assure you that anything you do that feeds a rivalry will corrupt your strength. As Theodore Roosevelt so aptly wrote, "Comparison is the thief of joy."

Anything you do that feeds a rivalry will corrupt your strength.

I certainly witnessed its theft that morning. I thought I was beyond this type of behavior. Really, I had not had this type of outburst in years! But that morning the combination of soul neglect and menopause proved to be combustible. It would appear that some of my life sources were muddied, and the garden of my heart was in desperate need of some attention. It looks like I had propped up some renegade vines when what they needed was a good dose of pruning.

Comparison has a pull to it. If allowed to, it will always move you away from your truest center. Comparison will attempt to puff you up through the insidious vehicle of pride, or it will push you down through the tyranny of insecurity. Either way it will not be long until you feel as though you are off kilter and on the outside looking in.

I hate seeing anyone intentionally left out. Yet there are times when feeling *on the outside* is the only thing that causes us to *look within*. I will say this about the list maker. She is young, witty, and smart. Whether I agree or disagree with her approach, I am very thankful for what the list exposed in me.

I fired a text off to my patient friend who was possibly questioning my sanity. Reentered my spouse's office to hug my holy husband. Marched my slippered feet off to my bedroom, closed the door, and hit my knees. The following is a portion of my prayer:

> *Heavenly Father,*
> *Thank you for exposing my flaws.*
> *Forgive me. Reveal the root of this weed. In the name of Jesus, amen.*

I went forward with my day and was actually able to look back on my hour of crazy and laugh at my absurdity. Later that day I met with my assistant. As we went through the mail, we discovered a rather unusual item. Apparently, I had been selected along with a few other women to make an appearance as honorary participants at a recent inspirational women's event. To honor us in our absence, they had created twelve-inch plastic laminated dolls of each of us. Mine had been sent to John in the hope that it might enjoy a spot in his office. As I turned the doll over in my hand, I laughed out loud while I made a mental note that white jeans were not my stage friends. I set it aside. I heard a familiar voice whisper, "You have been turned into a doll. Does this make you happy?"

I shook my head at my plastic image, dressed in white jeans with microphone in hand. The doll was as fake as the list. Again I laughed. I tried to throw away the doll, but my husband confiscated it, reminding me it had been sent to him, not to me. I suspect he keeps it to deter any more utterly absurd days in my near future.

The Three Cs

So how about those Scriptures, the ones John suggested, the ones I knew? First, there is 2 Corinthians 10:12:

> Not that we *dare to classify or compare* ourselves with some of those who are *commending* themselves. But when they measure themselves by one another and compare themselves with one another, they are without understanding.

Learn from me! Don't you *dare* classify, compare, or commend yourself. Why? It is an action of pride, even if the comparison you make is unfavorable. We all know pride is a precursor to a wipeout. And messing

Don't you dare classify, compare, or commend yourself.

87

with these three Cs will land you in a place that is at once dangerous and at times scary.

What Happens When We Classify

The wise do not classify. The wise do not want to be classified. Classifying people is not classy. To classify something is to put it in its place or assign it to a category. Some other terms for this word *classify* are to *grade*, *sort*, *brand*, *catalog*, *rank*, and perhaps the least desirable, *pigeonhole*. *Merriam-Webster's* describes this *pigeonhole* as "what is used to describe a neat category that usually fails to reflect actual complexities."

In life there are no neat categories. Life at its best is messy. The truth is that everyone's life is much more complex than what we see. And who in their right mind would want to be relegated to a box littered with pigeon fallout? Social media is but one of many opportunities we now enjoy that has the capacity to limit or expand both our prejudices and our perceptions.

In this day and age, it's not a bad idea to regularly ask, What do I ultimately want to be a part of building? Do I want to be ranked and graded and filed away with others? I know the list I read was an attempt to celebrate commonality . . . these women have arrived! It was created to celebrate something that hasn't always been celebrated . . . women ministering!

But when we look to be categorized, we may find ourselves contained. A wise older man warned my husband years ago, "Don't let them label you. If they can, then they will use the label in the future to one day disqualify you."

Let me just tell you most people do not grade on a curve. And those who have been harshly treated or left out will be oh so very happy to brand you as *less than.*

What Happens When We Compare

The brave do not dare to compare, even if that comparison sees them coming out on top. They realize that there are many more steps yet before them. They have glimpsed the eternal and realize that nothing earthbound can compare. This vision of a glorious *more* spurs them on. Comparison is a refuge for the cowardly who don't dare to believe there is something more.

What is the name of this mountain we climb? Popularity? From an eternal vantage point it is a pile of ashes. Or if we want to be more scriptural and quote Paul in Philippians 3:8, it's a pile of dog poop. Dung is not something to ascend; it is something to avoid and step over. The problem is too many of us are walking around with dog doo-doo on our feet, leaving a stinky trail in our wake. We have gotten used to the smell, but that doesn't mean it smells good. Philippians 3:7–9 reads:

> The very credentials these people are waving around as something special, I'm tearing up and throwing out with the trash—along with everything else I used to take credit for. And why? Because of Christ. Yes, all the things I once thought were so important are gone from my life. Compared to the high privilege of knowing Christ Jesus as my Master, firsthand, everything I once thought I had going for me is insignificant—dog dung. I've dumped it all in the trash so that I could embrace Christ and be embraced by him. (Message)

The opportunity to know Jesus as master is our highest privilege. When I reached for my phone rather than choosing to know him more, I chose the lesser thing.

It is far better to know God than to be known by man.

What Happens When We Commend

What about commending ourselves? What is wrong about occasionally celebrating what "we" have done? Yes, there is a time to celebrate and applaud growth. But this issue gets tangled when we treat what was freely given as though it was a personal achievement. Fruit is cultivated and gifts are merely received, and even then we're but stewards of God's gifts that are entrusted to us.

Some people are stunningly beautiful. Others are born into families with vast wealth and privilege. A rare few are born into both. Then there are those who are born into the very opposite circumstances. They live in dire poverty and are raised by families without any connections. There are those who lack an obvious outward beauty. Most of us fall into a place somewhere in the middle. And yet, none of these dynamics has the power to ultimately write your story or affect your value. God doesn't look at the outward appearance . . . he looks at the heart. The riches of one generation can sprout wings and abandon the next.

As I look at it, I think it's not fair, but this I know: God is just. He knows how to weigh the challenges and advantages of each and every soul in the palm of his hand. He alone holds the righteous measure. This is but one more reason why we should not compare. Because there is a very real eternal flip side to everything weighed here in the temporal realm.

This is where we get into some tight places and run the risk of modeling what honors man rather than what honors God, and when this dynamic is in play, we create unnecessary rivalries. Let's go ahead and pull the string and unravel the second half of 2 Corinthians 10:12:

> But when they measure themselves by one another and compare themselves with one another, they are without understanding.

You know I have done this. I would like to think we have all done this. We've measured and compared. There are those who arrogantly compare themselves with others, and then there are those who foolishly allow the comparison to diminish what God wants to do in their lives.

Pride imbalances one end of the spectrum, while insecurity cripples the other. Both extremes are dangerous. There is but one true measure, the immeasurable Christ, our anointed King of kings. He alone is holy, pure, and mighty. We are like an ant flexing outside our mound of dust foolishly imagining that the anteater is afraid to approach us, when all along the anteater trembles before the lion that we just happen to rest in the shadow of. No matter how industrious, how commendable we are, it is no match for the one who has remade us.

Here's another one of the Scriptures I could have turned to—John 5:44:

> How do you expect to get anywhere with God when you spend all your time jockeying for position with each other, ranking your rivals and ignoring God? (Message)

Why would we waste our time ranking our rivals when we have been invited into the presence of the unrivaled God?

Whenever I allow my life to be defined by people, I find my connection with my heavenly Father slipping. Soon my vantage point is distorted by what I see and hear people say about who I am, and I forget God's declaration of who I am becoming. There are times I wonder just how much my foolish actions and limited understanding have consequences beyond my understanding.

I hope that you can laugh at my ridiculous morning and arrest any of your own tendencies toward comparison. It would be exhausting if this was not just a onetime occasion but a daily dynamic. The reason comparison isn't a constant in my life is because I have people like my husband and faithful friend who jerk the slack out of me.

Biting and Devouring

Social media is a way of inviting many people and voices into your world. This can be a good thing, but it does make a lot of unfriendly people our neighbors. If you cannot love them, perhaps it would be better for you to put some boundaries back in place. If someone is hateful, don't answer them back in the same manner; raise the bar. Living under grace does not license us to be rude to one another. It does not say you shall compare your neighbor with yourself and make sure you always come out ahead.

Paul wrote, "For the whole law is fulfilled in one word: 'You shall love your neighbor as yourself.' But if you bite and devour one another, watch out that you are not consumed by one another" (Gal. 5:14–15). The picture here is not a pretty one. Two people taking chunks out of each other like ravenous, senseless beasts until both are consumed is not what we should model as those who profess Christ. And yet this is what some of our blogging and electronic verbal sparring looks like. Maybe this carnage is not apparent on your phone or a website, but it is definitely bloody in the spirit. There didn't used to be such easy access to people. Now you can be biting and devouring in a blink of an eye. Sadly, I know because I have done it.

What I growl and bite at usually reveals the areas that yet need work in me. If someone hits a tender spot, my default is to guard the wound. I've learned to put my phone down and walk away from it as though it were a loaded gun. There are many times that people are just having a bad day. Cut them some slack.

There is a vast difference between inspiring others and inciting jealousy. Just as there is a vast difference between inviting others in and intentionally making others feel left out. If you are following someone on social media and they are bringing out the worst in you, rather than blaming it on them, perhaps you should take a step back and ask yourself, "Why?"

Rivalry will rob you unless you learn how to turn what the enemy meant for bad into what God can use for good. The following Scripture reveals what environments that are rife with rivalry look like:

> It is obvious what kind of life develops out of trying to get your own way all the time: repetitive, loveless, cheap sex; a stinking accumulation of mental and emotional garbage; frenzied and joyless grabs for happiness; trinket gods; magic-show religion; paranoid loneliness; cutthroat competition;

all-consuming-yet-never-satisfied wants; a brutal temper; an impotence to love or be loved; divided homes and divided lives; small-minded and lopsided pursuits; *the vicious habit of depersonalizing everyone into a rival*; uncontrolled and uncontrollable addictions; ugly parodies of community. I could go on. This isn't the first time I have warned you, you know. *If you use your freedom this way, you will not inherit God's kingdom.* (Gal. 5:19–21 Message)

I actually want to weep just reading these words. Lately there has been far too much of the very things Paul listed for us here. And I am not pointing a finger at our world; Galatians is a letter to the church. What does it mean to *depersonalize* someone? It is a way of stripping someone of their personhood. It deprives them of their individuality and unique personality. The Nazis depersonalized the Jews until the German people no longer saw individuals made in the image of God . . . they saw a collective problem that did not reflect their Aryan image. Sadly, this tactic is still in use in our day, both for groups and for individuals.

People are far too quick to resort to judging and name-calling. People have hearts, and whether you realize it or not, electronic words still wound. As Aesop observed, "It is easy to be brave from a safe distance." Many of our social media formats create "a safe distance." This dynamic serves to embolden the cowardly or critical with a means to bully and slander the people they have depersonalized. They would never dare to say these things to another person face-to-face. Why? Because it is hard to pretend someone is a robot when you see the tears in their eyes. I have watched as Christians called one another everything from heretics to whores . . .

while Satan just laughed. The more we do his work, the less he has to do.

How to Rebuke and Correct

Some of you may even now be arguing, "But shouldn't those who are wrong be publicly corrected?" Well, the good news is that God has an app for that:

> Better is open rebuke than hidden love. Faithful are the wounds of a friend; profuse are the kisses of an enemy. (Prov. 27:5–6)

What does this Scripture mean when it encourages *open* rebuke? The key to this is the word *open*. It works best with open hearts, open arms, and open faces. We all should correct others the way we would want to hear correction. Ideally, I want to be corrected by people who bring out the best in me.

This Scripture is highlighting correction between friends, but it could be a leader, teacher, or employer as well. Because all correction has a better chance of being received when it comes directly from someone who knows or deeply cares about you. It is ideal if this interaction can happen one-on-one. If an in-person encounter can't happen, then a phone call is the next best option.

(As an aside, I would not recommend texting correction. Too much can be lost in translation. Texting provides no body language cues and no tone of voice. John and I have experienced a lot of ridiculous miscommunication when we texted each other. One of us, usually me, will put something in all caps for EMPHASIS that will be misinterpreted as YELLING!)

We have all experienced the closed rebuke; it is when people correct you behind your back. When people navigate the need for your correction without your involvement, you need to question the sincerity of their rebuke. While they could be correct in what they say, it will not help you grow unless you are included in the process.

Actually, this type of correction usually hurts the growth process, because when people speak about you behind your back, they set you up to react defensively. The face-to-face "open rebuke" of a genuine friend gives both people involved the chance to respond to each other and grow through the process of correction.

Correcting someone on social media channels is *not* an open rebuke just because it is open to the public. I have beautiful, strong friends I love and respect. These are the very ones with whom I am close enough to know the manner in which they live their lives. I have watched these same godly people be openly attacked by other people who have never bothered to come to them with their concerns but instead have publicly brandished their distortion of truth to wound my friends. The Bible is very clear on this topic:

> As for a person who stirs up division, after warning him once and then twice, *have nothing more to do with him*, knowing that such a person is warped and sinful; he is self-condemned. (Titus 3:10–11)

Don't read their blogs, join their arguments, follow them on Twitter, friend them on Facebook . . . nothing. It is not healthy for you. Look for inspiration, not division.

In The Message, Titus 3:10–11 reads:

Warn a quarrelsome person once or twice, but then be done with him. It's obvious that such a person is out of line, rebellious against God. By persisting in divisiveness he cuts himself off.

As I have moved through life, my friends have become fewer but truer. My friends show me who I want to be, while my enemies reveal who I don't want to be. An environment that breeds rivalry might bring out the worst in us at first. When we find ourselves flailing, God can get involved and use the struggle to develop character in us.

The next verse in Proverbs 27 offers a better way:

One who is full loathes honey, but to one who is hungry everything bitter is sweet. (v. 7)

I'm hungry to see more of the fruit of godliness in my life. I am hungry to grow more. The closer I get to God, the more I see what obstructs his life in me. Some of the sweetest things I have experienced in life are friends who cared enough to wound me with the truth. Enemies may flatter or they may wound us with lies. Let's not be satisfied with human lists and comparisons. When we notice the pangs of inadequacy that rivalry inflicts or the smugness and isolation of pride, let's hit our knees. If we go to our Father, he will be more than happy to remove what keeps us from getting closer to him.

Discussion Questions

1. Have you been labeled or pigeonholed? (Examples may be gender, race, or age limits.) How have these labels

limited you? How can you move yourself out beyond this classification?

2. In what areas of life is comparison robbing your joy?

3. When we classify, compare, and commend, what is it really a deeper sign of? (Hint: Proverbs 29:25.)

4. Is social media inspiring or inciting you? What steps can you take to make sure it is a constructive influence?

5. Explain the difference between the approach and motives of a closed rebuke versus an open rebuke.

5

When You're Seen as a Rival

A certain amount of opposition is a great help
to a man. Kites rise against, not with, the wind.

Lewis Mumford

I was recently on the phone with a dear friend. Her husband is a gifted musician and music producer, and she is a powerful minister and an all-around astounding individual. I've always known them to be pure, humble, and compassionate, yet they'd been through a lot recently. They'd been maligned, rejected, and misjudged.

My friend explained, "They have slandered us to . . ." at which point she shared the names of a few key players. I listened. I understood. Then I lost track of what she was saying, because I no longer saw where they'd been or even what they were presently going through. I saw where the future would take them. I got so excited about what I saw that I blurted out, "Good! You need to thank God for them. Their harsh treatment has made you into who you are today."

Understand, it was not their mistreatment that I was celebrating; it was this couple's response to the mistreatment that made me know their future was bright.

Of course it was easy for me to say this while I was on the outside looking in. Then I included myself in the celebration and affirmed, "I have learned to be so incredibly *thankful* for the opposition of rivals in my life."

That conversation was just what I needed that day. It encouraged me on what had been a hard day for me as well. I hope none of you will ever be judged harshly and called a heretic. If you have been, then you know it hurts.

But rather than quit and wallow in the despair of discouragement, I have learned to look back and see the repeated faithfulness of God. He carried me each and every time when I didn't think I could go on another day. I have learned more about the faithfulness of God from my enemies than from my friends. I will go even further; I have learned more about myself from my enemies than from my friends.

Friends will offer you shelter. Which is a good thing, but not necessarily a dynamic that fosters growth. Friends want to see you protected from the storms of life, while an enemy will do their best to lock you out in the pouring rain. But what if you are in a season when God wants you to learn that he is your ultimate shelter? Who is a better instructor: a rival or a friend?

Rivals are a fact of life. I know. Sorry. I don't like it either, but it is true. And yet rivals are not without purpose. Creating a life without rival is not about removing rivals from your life. Rather, it is about understanding that truly all things can work together for our good when we are called according to God's purpose. We can use the dynamics of rivalry to spur us on to greater growth and insight.

If viewed correctly, rivals can serve as a catalyst, exposing our weaknesses and challenging us to develop our strengths. They push us beyond our limits and cause us to look up when we feel alone.

Maybe you are thinking, wait—you just told me I am a daughter without rival, an heiress of unrivaled promise, created to worship a God without rival.

All true. You are a daughter without rival in the eyes of God. This is how you should see yourself *relationally* with your Creator, and it is your vantage point for how you *relate* to others. But we would be more than naïve if we pretended that rivalries didn't exist and that the promises came to us without a battle. The proclamation "You are the light of the world" (Matt. 5:14) does not negate the existence of darkness. Saying that you are a daughter without rival does not mean you will not encounter rivals any more than saying you are light means you will never face darkness.

The word *rival* expresses itself in three distinct ways: as a noun, an adjective, and a verb.

Right away basic grammar tells us a rival can *be* a person, place, or thing; can *describe* a person, place, or thing; and lastly can be the *actions* of a person, place, or thing. As a noun, the word *rival* ranges in meaning all the way from lighthearted terms that denote a peer, equal, or competitor into the darker realm of adversary, enemy, or foe. As an adjective, the word *rival* captures everything from the challenges of competing with a friend to the struggle of contending with an enemy. And lastly, as a verb, *rival*'s definition ranges from the benign—to match, resemble, or compare—to dominance: surpass, confront, and exceed.

Rivals are real. Chances are high that even now someone sees *you* as their rival and you are yet unaware. Most people don't knowingly sign up to be rivals unless they are competing in sports, academics, pageants, science fairs, or an election. You don't go to work expecting to encounter rivals, and you certainly don't expect to find them at church! However, rivals appear in every part of life, and you have minimal control over how others ultimately choose to see you. Sorry. Even if you were to hire the best PR firm to interact with the public on your behalf, you would still only be managing their perceptions. The sooner you accept this, the better. The good news is you have complete control over how *you* choose to see *others*. And there are very real times that changing the way you see others radically changes the way they see you. I'll get into that more in a later chapter.

Regardless what a rival's motives are, you can always flip a rivalry to your advantage. All you have to do is remember these two key things about control.

1. You can't control and are not responsible for what others say, think, do, or feel.
2. You can control and are responsible for what *you* say, think, do, or feel.

We all know what rivals can do *to us*, but in this section I want to unpack what rivals can actually do *for us*.

Rivals Reveal God's Power

Hidden away at birth, rescued by royalty, raised in the house of Pharaoh, Moses had a life of intrigue from the very beginning. God used these factors to preserve Moses's life. But like us, Moses learned that *destiny is revealed in seasons of confrontation rather than seasons of comfort.*

Moses learned this the hard way when he tried to take matters into his own hands only to find himself exiled from his people and all he had ever known. I imagine his sojourn in the desert felt very much like a long, nomadic time-out. Then suddenly,

Destiny is revealed in seasons of confrontation rather than seasons of comfort.

God tapped Moses when he was on the backside of the desert living as a refugee. There is a lesson here. Just because you mishandled something in the past doesn't mean it is hands-off in your future. Moses knew why his life had been preserved and had a sense of what God was calling him to do and be, but he lacked the character of a deliverer. God needed to cultivate a depth in Moses, one that life in the palace could never develop. God prepares us in secret for what we will one day face publicly. The day came when a very different Moses was restored to his brother Aaron, sister Miriam, and his people Israel. In the fullness of time, God anointed him as a deliverer and ambassador to meet Pharaoh.

God was about to position Moses at a place of world prominence by forcing him into the presence of his rival, Pharaoh. Even as God sends Moses to Pharaoh, he lets him know that Pharaoh will not heed his voice:

You shall speak all that I command you, and your brother Aaron shall tell Pharaoh to let the people of Israel go out of his land. But I will harden Pharaoh's heart, and though I multiply my signs and wonders in the land of Egypt, Pharaoh will not listen to you. Then I will lay my hand on Egypt and bring my hosts, my people the children of Israel, out of the land of Egypt by great acts of judgment. The Egyptians shall know that I am the LORD, when I stretch out my hand against Egypt and bring out the people of Israel from among them. (Exod. 7:2–5)

God had a purpose in what looked like a doomed mission. The very reason Pharaoh had his position of prominence was to magnify God to the people of the earth:

For by now I could have put out my hand and struck you and your people with pestilence, and you would have been cut off from the earth. But for this purpose I have raised you [Pharaoh] up, to show you my power, so that my name may be proclaimed in all the earth. (Exod. 9:15–16)

Rivals reveal God's power. The conflict with Egypt served to elevate and distinguish an oppressed people group who worshiped a God without form or name in a nation of idol worshipers. What conflict might God be using even now to distinguish his hand on your life and release you—and others— from oppression? Look carefully at what fights against your destiny and see if you don't perceive the gift of a rival in your midst.

Who made King David famous? Was it a prophet, a father, or a friend? No, it was a rival: Goliath.

Without this face-to-face confrontation with a Philistine rival, David could have remained in a wilderness of obscurity. He was, after all, the youngest brother in a family of eight sons. Even though David was anointed to be king by the prophet Samuel, there still remained a series of rivals to navigate before he became king. The anointing sets you apart, but confrontations with Goliath will set you up.

When Goliath presented himself on the battlefield, it was likely an attempt to engage Saul. Saul was Israel's champion, a skilled warrior, even though he was not as tall as Goliath. The Bible says that Saul was head and shoulders taller than the other men of Israel. Scholars estimate Saul's height as between 6′ and 6′6″. Goliath, on the other hand, was over nine feet tall.

Either way, the warrior Goliath towered over King Saul. And King Saul towered over the shepherd David. But David had something that made up for his lack of height. David had "grit." If someone has grit, it means they have pluck, courage, determination, and resolve. A recent study reported that this element called "grit" was a better determiner of which cadets would graduate from West Point than SAT scores or academic ranking.[1] The study included a self-assessment that ranked a personal grit factor on a scale from 1 to 5.

I'm pretty sure David was a 5+. You don't tangle with a lion or a bear without some serious grit in play. He had too much grit to doubt the outcome of facing a giant. Saul was taller, but I'm pretty sure he ran shorter than David in the grit department. No one becomes a legend without grit. There is nothing epic about winning an equally matched fight. There needed to be enough disparity that all those who were involved were caught off guard. The observers needed to walk away and say, "I didn't see that coming, but that was awesome." David needed a rival who was colossal enough to put him on the map. The renown of the famous but hesitant warrior Saul and the terror of the Philistines' champion positioned David to be a warrior without rival.

In *David and Goliath*, author Malcolm Gladwell astutely points out:

> Much of what we consider valuable in our world arises out of these kinds of lopsided conflicts, because the act of facing overwhelming odds produces greatness and beauty. . . . Being an underdog can change people in ways that we often fail to appreciate: it can open doors and create opportunities and educate and enlighten and make possible what might otherwise have seemed unthinkable.[2]

When you are positioned to face an impossible rival, you have two choices: surrender and yield, or rise to your full stature and call on that gritty something bigger within you.

David shook off the confinement of King Saul's armor and called on the name of his God:

> Then David said to the Philistine, "You come to me with a sword and with a spear and with a javelin, but *I come to you in the name of the LORD of hosts, the God of the armies of Israel*, whom you have defied. This day the LORD will deliver you into my hand, and I will strike you down and cut off your head. And I will give the dead bodies of the host of the Philistines this day to the birds of the air and to the wild beasts of the earth, *that all the earth may know that there is a God in Israel.* (1 Sam. 17:45–46)

Not only did Goliath massively position David for his destiny, but this victory over the Philistine also let the *entire earth* know that God's hand was upon Israel. Like David, I know you are hungry to make God famous. There are yet Goliaths in our world. They challenge us and defy the existence of our God. These giants masquerade as bullies in school, work, and public opinion. It is time we stop hiding behind rocks and run forward with the Word of God in our mouths.

You are filled with the same Spirit that raised Christ from the grave. Rivals want you to fight on their terms and in your own strength. You must not. You must be bigger than that. As children without rival, we do good when we are dealt evil. Ultimately, this is not about our glory; it is all for his.

Goliath made David famous. Social media can make someone famous. But fame is not what makes someone a king. If misused, fame serves to feed egotistical dictators rather than build servants. God did not want another insecure leader who led like Saul. He needed someone who would worship him and openly display his power. We are commissioned as kings and priests unto our God. Our allegiance is to our Lord, not to the popularity of people. David feared God; Saul feared the people.

The flip side of famous means you have fans . . . not disciples or followers. Fans can be fickle. They love you one moment and hate you the next. King David didn't need fans. He needed men and women who would pledge their lives. Godly kings need wise counselors, a loyal army, and faithful servants. To draw this kind of following, David would require some refining. God had another rival positioned to prepare David for kingship.

Rivals Reveal Your Destiny

Rivals have the power to pull you out of obscurity or knock you out of your place of prominence. The good news is that you get to choose what they will produce in your life. Will your rival best you . . . or bring out the best in you? For this very reason a rival can also reveal your destiny.

Will your rival best you . . . or bring out the best in you?

David had known God in the capacity of son and shepherd. Surrounded by sheep, he had worshiped God under the brilliant light of Middle Eastern stars. In a shepherd's wilderness, he had confronted the lion and the bear and rescued his sheep. Now David would learn what it meant to be attacked and driven away like a wild animal.

King Saul was perfectly wired to drive gritty David from the presence of people into the presence of God; this is where David would receive his anointing and where his destiny as king would be revealed.

The relationship between Saul and David did not begin as it ended. At first, Saul loved David and recognized God's hand on his life. Saul drew David close when he felt vulnerable and tormented and entrusted David with matters of the kingdom. Here's what 1 Samuel 18:5 tells us:

> Whatever Saul gave David to do, he did it—and did it well. So well that Saul put him in charge of his military operations. Everybody, both the people in general and Saul's servants, approved of and admired David's leadership. (Message)

Saul couldn't ask for a better general. And when an evil spirit vexed Saul, David would play the harp and sing to quiet his soul. Everything was going smoothly until King Saul heard another song. You probably know the story:

As they returned home, after David had killed the Philistine, the women poured out of all the villages of Israel singing and dancing, welcoming King Saul with tambourines, festive songs, and lutes. In playful frolic the women sang, *Saul kills by the thousand, David by the ten thousand!*

This made Saul angry—very angry. He took it as a personal insult. He said, "They credit David with 'ten thousands' and me with only 'thousands.' Before you know it they'll be giving him the kingdom!" From that moment on, Saul kept his eye on David. (1 Sam. 18:6–9 Message)

Even if neither of these men literally killed in these numbers, Saul was offended by the comparison. It was as though the women's song opened Saul's eyes, and then he opened his mouth and prophesied his own demise. The women were singing the song as a tease, but it was far from funny to Saul. It hit a nerve. Years had passed since the prophet had told Saul that his disobedience had cost him the kingdom. Samuel declared it would be torn from him and given to another who was his better (1 Sam. 15:28). With this song the fabric of Saul's life began to tear. In a split second, he was overcome with foreboding as he recognized David as his replacement. Saul had no intentions of stepping aside peacefully.

When you are dealing with insecurity, an unfavorable comparison can change a friend into a rival in the blink of an eye. Saul no longer saw David as the asset he had proven himself to be; he saw David as a threat, and everything shifted overnight:

The next day a harmful spirit from God rushed upon Saul, and he raved within his house while David was playing the lyre, as he did day by day. (1 Sam. 18:10)

This messes with a bit of our theology and serves as a reminder for all of us . . . God can use whatever he wants to achieve his purpose. In this case, it meant sending an agent of torment to push an envious king over the edge.

On this day David was just doing what he had always done, playing the lyre, but now Saul had something different in his hand because something had shifted in his heart.

> Saul had his spear in his hand. And Saul hurled the spear, for he thought, "I will pin David to the wall." But David evaded him twice. (vv. 10–11)

Picture the contrast here. Saul stormed through his house, weapon in his hand, while David peacefully played an instrument of worship. Can the contrast be more vast? Who runs around their house with a spear? Saul had gone caveman.

Because I have written on the subject of swords, I have a number of swords in various places in my house, but rarely do any of them find their way into my hand. Not even on my worst flipped-out hormone days would I dare to lift one. Because when you are under pressure, you're tempted to throw whatever is in your hand. (I speak from experience.) David was now forced to take evasive action to avoid the very same man who yesterday rode by his side and had his back in battle. David's *best* brought out Saul's *worst*, and the nagging foreboding progressed to a fully formed spirit of fear.

> Now *Saul feared David. It was clear that God was with David and had left Saul.* So, Saul got David out of his sight by making him an officer in the army. David was in combat frequently. Everything David did turned out well. Yes, GOD

was with him. As Saul saw David becoming more successful, he himself grew more fearful. (1 Sam. 18:12–15 Message)

David's military successes should have been celebrated as King Saul's victories. But rather than seeing these exploits as David securing the kingdom under the leadership of Saul, Saul imagined each battle stripped his authority away. Saul no longer saw David as a son, nor did his company comfort him. He wanted David out of his sight. And yet his reasoning didn't stop there. Out of sight, out of mind was not going to work in this case. King Saul put David in combat hoping he would lose his life. Once again, this only served to position David to flourish. David rose as Saul tried to bury him:

> As Saul more and more realized that GOD was with David, and how much his own daughter, Michal, loved him, *his fear of David increased and settled into hate. Saul hated David.* (1 Sam. 18:28–29)

In a very short span of time, Saul's perception of David had morphed from suspicion to fear to hate. Gone was the David who was considered a beloved son, military hero, and ally. David was now branded an outlaw. His short-lived season of favor in the courts of Saul had come to an end. Alarmed by this shift that came without any provocation on his part, David fled for his life.

This departure from the king's court began an entirely new season in David's life. Rather than status and reward, this one was filled with constant rejection, harsh treatment, and desperate danger in the wilderness. Some scholars place this time period at about eight years. It was in exile and barren rocky expanses that David learned the lessons that would prepare him to be a king after God's own heart.

David was being hunted down by a ravenous wolf that drove him from cave to cave. He grieved when he heard how Saul had slaughtered the priests and their families only because they had unknowingly helped him. Over the course of years of anguish, Saul's rivalry with David helped David know, whether he was in a palace or a cave, it was the development of godliness that mattered. David was facing his second Goliath.

Allow me to explain.

I don't think it is too much of a stretch to say that David may have had some father issues. Each time David interacted with the king in the wilderness, he cried out and called Saul "father." First Samuel 24:11 is a window into his anguish:

> *See, my father*, see the corner of your robe in my hand. For by the fact that I cut off the corner of your robe and did not kill you, you may know and see that there is no wrong or treason in my hands. *I have not sinned against you, though you hunt my life to take it.*

There is no reason to think malice existed between David and his father, but as the eighth son, David might have been easy to overlook. It would appear that David was somewhat lost in the shadow of his seven older brothers. Like all sons, David would have hoped for his father's affirmation and recognition, and yet his father failed to send for him when the prophet Samuel came to anoint the sons of Jesse:

> And Jesse made seven of his sons pass before Samuel. And Samuel said to Jesse, "The LORD has not chosen these." Then

Samuel said to Jesse, "Are all your sons here?" And he said, "There remains yet the youngest, but behold, he is keeping the sheep." And Samuel said to Jesse, "Send and get him, for we will not sit down till he comes here." (1 Sam. 16:10–11)

Why did Samuel have to ask if there was yet another son? You would think that Jesse would have sent for David when Samuel first arrived. Jesse must not have seen David as in the running for the position of chosen. If Samuel the prophet came to our house, I would do everything within my power to be certain that my *entire* family was present. I would Skype, FaceTime, or call them in so that if any weren't present they would be accounted for.

David had seven rivals for his father's attention, his brothers. The interactions that Scripture has recorded between David and his brothers do not paint a picture of warmth and support. In fact, his oldest brother accused him of pride, belittled his role in his father's house, and called his heart presumptuous and evil (1 Sam. 17:28).

This may be the reason why when I read the psalms of David I don't hear words . . . I hear heart. Woven within the stanzas I see the agony born of years of isolation and exhaustion. David proved his innocence repeatedly to Saul, and yet the battle continued to rage.

At some point David realized his innocence would never be recognized in the courts of men. Saul would never pardon David. God alone would do this. In running and hiding from Saul, David learned to run and hide *in* God. Many people want to be anointed, but they forget that the anointing comes with a purpose that is worked out in the presence of their enemies.

Later in life when David was running from Absalom, he cried out,

> Lord, how are they increased that trouble me!
>   many are they that rise up against me.
> Many there be which say of my soul,
> There is no help for him in God. Selah.
> But thou, O LORD, art a shield for me;
>   my glory, and the lifter up of mine head.
> I cried unto the LORD with my voice,
>   and he heard me out of his holy hill. Selah.
> I laid me down and slept;
> I awaked; for the LORD sustained me.
> I will not be afraid of ten thousands of people,
>   that have set themselves against me round about.
>   (Ps. 3:1–6 KJV)

How were they increased that troubled him? Good question. Why didn't God just shut them down? Perhaps bury them all in a desert sandstorm?

David did not ask to be anointed as king by the prophet Samuel. Gritty David could not help but be valiant for his God. As he was a faithful son with what was entrusted to him by his Father, so he was a faithful warrior to his king. Jonathan could not have asked for a truer friend. So far as his actions were concerned, David was blameless. And yet throughout his life trouble increased. Why?

We want there to be a reason, because if there is one, this mess might make sense. But it all appears to be senseless. These words were lived and prophesied by David—and his struggle identified the battles of another: they reached into the future and revealed what would happen to Jesus. Why are we surprised when rivals arise in our life? First Peter 4:12–13 reminds us:

> Beloved, do not be surprised at the fiery trial when it comes upon you to test you, as though something strange were happening to you. But rejoice insofar as you share Christ's sufferings, that you may also rejoice and be glad when his glory is revealed.

Outward pressure works inward transformation. Rivals reveal the destiny that God has prepared for us. We decrease that God's glory might increase in our lives. The gift of a rival is part of the learning, refining, training package. It is human nature to want to avoid hardship. But when we suffer, not only do we share in Jesus's pain, but we also partake of his glory as he reveals our destiny to us.

Rivals Force You to Guard Your Heart

As your heart of stone is broken, a heart of flesh appears. When you find yourself involved in a senseless rivalry, your heart feels assaulted. You are bombarded with questions that cause you to second-guess yourself and your motives. You wonder, Is there something wrong with me? God, where are you? How did this happen? Why does this keep on happening?

Often the only answer we receive to these questions is silence. We begin to question whether God hears us. I have come to learn he is quiet when there is an intermission. The scene is about to change, and the characters are finding their places on set. Be encouraged. Your season is about to transition. Rather than measuring yourself by where you are, remember what he has already brought you through.

As we listen in silence, we are poised for a transition. Will we believe what God has said, or will we heed what our rival accusers are saying? The same God who began this good work in us will be faithful to complete it. Will we allow the attacks to harden our hearts, or will we allow God to heal? Will we focus our attention on the words of an enemy or on the words of our Creator?

> **Will we allow the attacks to harden our hearts, or will we allow God to heal?**

> Dear friend, listen well to my words; tune your ears to my voice.
>
> Keep my message in plain view at all times. Concentrate! Learn it by heart! Those who discover these words live, really live; body and soul, they're bursting with health. Keep vigilant watch over your heart; that's where life starts. (Prov. 4:20–23 Message)

Don't watch what they are doing. Don't listen to what they are saying. Don't compare your current state with theirs. Guard your heart and every promise that has been whispered into the recesses of your soul. Remove yourself from the static and develop your ability to become in tune with God's voice. He would not encourage you to do this if he did not long to speak to you. His voice holds fast your heart.

In this life there is so much static. The vibrant, unrivaled God-life you long for will not be found by way of casual pursuit. It requires concentration in a world bombarded with distractions. If you are not intentional, you will be diverted by the many distractions that vie for your attention.

The message of Christ is our ultimate focus. The words of our Creator hold the power to bring forth what is written upon our lives. This intentional convergence by the very source of life aligns body and soul and positions our lives to surge with health, purpose, and power. When we concentrate on his Word, instead of our rivals, we enter into a life beyond their grasp.

Not only are we to concentrate on his Word, which is like seed, but we are also to watch over the garden, which is our heart.

There is a vast difference between *guarding* your heart and *an imprisoned* heart. One keeps vigil over an item of great value; the other could be likened to a heart on lockdown.

Too many choose to harden their hearts in the hope this will keep their hearts protected until later when they feel it is safe to let them heal. Growing up I often chose this tactic. At first, the sense of relief was enormous. I would cut people off when they hurt me. I slammed the door of my heart so often that I found myself safely locked away. I shut off my heart until I made it my prisoner. I imagined myself impervious to pain only to realize too late that I was likewise numb to joy.

Guarding your heart is protecting it rather than imprisoning it. If you have put your heart on lockdown, make time for prayer. Ask God to release your heart from its stony prison and replace your heart with one that feels both joy and pain.

I know it hurts, but don't shut off your tears. Let them water your heart and keep it tender. Don't drown your pain in drugs or alcohol, which distort your senses and cause you to fall. Don't darken your mind with thoughts of revenge,

117

which blacken your soul. Stop overthinking this, sit down, and cry as often as you need to. Be alone, let the pain hit you full force. When the calm descends, turn your face toward heaven and lift your voice to God. Follow the pattern of David and develop the daily practice of entrusting your soul, your cause, and your rivals to God. Psalm 51:8–12 captures it all:

> Let me hear joy and gladness;
>> let the bones that you have broken rejoice.
> Hide your face from my sins,
>> and blot out all my iniquities.
> Create in me a clean heart, O God,
>> and renew a right spirit within me.
> Cast me not away from your presence,
>> and take not your Holy Spirit from me.
> Restore to me the joy of your salvation,
>> and uphold me with a willing spirit.

A hardened, captive heart becomes deaf, and bound bones can't respond. Those who judge others live constantly under the weight of their own sin. God alone can cleanse what dirties our hearts and right what was wrong so that we rise again upright in his presence.

Hardened hearts do not stand in the presence of God. They isolate themselves or recline in the company of scorners who mock the pain of those who have chosen the tender path of healing.

Again I warn you, many begin with this approach only to discover too late that their hearts were not guarded; they were imprisoned. Empathy and compassion leave, and cruelty and indifference take up residence. There is a vast difference between guarding what is sacred and locking away your heart.

When our hearts feel empty and barren, it is time to fill our mouths with song. Saul was too tormented to sing over himself, so David sang for Saul to keep his suffering at bay. Songs that surround us will keep something at a distance, but something truly significant happens when a song rises within us. As we sing rather than merely listen, our hearts are unlocked and a connection is made with our Creator.

King Saul had a history of both speaking and acting rashly. The turbulence in his heart was expressed in his actions. Just as David learned to quiet his heart, we can learn to quiet ours:

> I've kept my feet on the ground, I've cultivated a quiet heart.
> Like a baby content in its mother's arms, my soul is a baby content. (Ps. 131:2 Message)

Can I share something rather embarrassing? Rather than quiet my soul like a baby, I have a tendency to act like one. Decades ago our church would sing the words of Psalm 3 in our worship services. My response was to cry like a baby. At home I had been known to dance to the song. Somehow I likened my mourning to what David was feeling when he wrote the psalm. The only problem was the things I was crying about were minor infractions. Yes. They felt major at the time. I was sure they had pierced me so deep they had rent my soul.

Looking back I see it differently. The infractions were petty and pitiful. A slight here, unkind words there, perhaps a fight with my husband. I have met so many who would give anything for these types of infractions. Overseas I have met brave women who live daily with the threat of death for their faith. Everywhere I turn I meet strong single mothers who labor tirelessly to provide for their children. Not to mention those who have been beaten, raped, sold by family members, and trafficked.

I am not belittling your pain. I know it is real. But when we truly get a revelation of how our God turns even the worst situation to his advantage, then the day will come when like Joseph we can say:

> As for you, you meant evil against me, but God meant it for good. (Gen. 50:20)

If you change your perspective on your rivals, God will redeem your pain. The playwright Edmond Burke captured the dynamic this way: "He that struggles with us strengthens our nerves, and sharpens our skill. Our antagonist is our helper."

I have learned that closing doors to others translates to closed doors in our future. Whenever we try to isolate others, we run the risk of excluding ourselves. Open hearts will open doors and welcome others with open arms. God sent Jesus in the hope that none would be left out. Do the hard work with your heart, guard it well rather than guarding what you think is your position.

Many want to be a leader, but having a measure of influence is a two-edged sword that cuts both ways. There will always be people who love you but don't know you. There will also be those who hate you but don't know you. These are the spectators. They are not your rivals, but they watch the interchange. Moses grew up with Pharaoh. David had been like a son to Saul. (Goliath was just one of life's giants.) In most cases, a rival is someone who once knew you well. David described a rival this way:

For it is not an enemy who taunts me—then I could bear it; it is not an adversary who deals insolently with me—then I could hide from him.

But it is you, a man, my equal, my companion, my familiar friend.

We used to take sweet counsel together; within God's house we walked in the throng. (Ps. 55:12–14)

Today we might call this a "frenemy," which the Urban dictionary describes as "an enemy disguised as a friend." More simply put, it is a rival. It is a gift to be able to discern who our true friends are, yet at the same time it is often our rivals who ultimately make us true. We can argue our case, or we can lay it before God. We can thank God that he is using a rival to refine or reposition us, or we can whine. We can complain, or we can pray and sing. The choice is ours to make, and no rival can take that away from us.

Discussion Questions

1. Recount a time when a rival became your instructor.
2. What has a rival exposed in your life?
3. What are some areas where you are gritty?
4. What are some not-so-gritty areas that need to be strengthened?
5. Name three differences between fans and followers.
6. Have you been running through your house with a spear in your hand? How might you put it down?
7. How can you guard your heart without imprisoning it?

6

Gender without Rival

I cannot be opposed to racism, in which people
are discriminated against as a result of something about which they can do nothing—their
skin color—and then accept with equanimity the
gross injustice of penalizing others for something
else they can do nothing about—their gender.

Archbishop Desmond Tutu

I have private prayers, ones I pray when I am alone. More
often than not *alone* translates to a hotel room or my
car. I have been known to pray some pretty unusual ones
while in the bubble of my vehicle. There is nothing better
than when the worship music is blaring and I am fully in
the moment. A few years ago my life was on the fast-spin
cycle. At times, I didn't know if I was coming or going. My
book *Lioness Arising* had released in the fall while I was in
the nation of Jordan. The year was coming to a close and

Thanksgiving was nearly upon us. My private prayer at the time went something like this:

"Heavenly Father, I bet you know I released a book called *Lioness Arising*. It has already been published in five languages, but I would love to know that this was your will. I know it is after the fact, but I also know you're independent of time, so I'd love a confirmation that this is something you ordained. In Jesus's name, amen." Yes, this is somewhat embarrassing but nonetheless true. I knew I had to get it off my heart and into his hands.

Well, the requested confirmation did not take long. That night around eight o'clock I found myself unexpectedly in the midst of a school project with my youngest son. I had torn apart his older brother's school projects for things we could use when he informed me that he needed a specific type of poster board to complete this project. I braved a blizzard to access the correct poster board but not before agreeing to pay the older brothers to help him complete the project. I returned home to mayhem—magazine scraps, markers, and letters littered our family table. One brother was typing out what Arden dictated while another was cutting out the pictures to be glued. I had just laid out the board that would unite all the pieces when the phone rang. It was John.

He sounded excited. I felt overwhelmed.

He explained he had met someone that very night whom I needed to talk to. My husband has a regular habit of putting me on the phone with complete strangers. I am not sure how it happens, but it happens . . . a lot. These are people who probably have no interest in talking to me, but John gets caught up in the moment and feels I must speak to them.

At first, I fought these introductions. But now I feel they are simply inevitable. Word to the wise: if your husband has an annoying habit for more than ten years, you need to decide it is cute. So my husband has a cute habit of putting me on the phone with strangers. But that night I protested.

"John, I do not have time to talk to strangers. I am in the throes of a school project with Arden."

"That's okay, you don't have to talk to him right now. He is a military officer—he's busy now so I gave him your number. Be sure to answer when he calls later tonight. Gotta go, love you!" and before I could argue further he was gone.

The work on the project intensified. Within an hour my phone rang. I decided to answer in my best exhausted voice.

"Hello," I droned.

The caller seemed hesitant.

"Is this Lisa Bevere?"

"Yes . . ."

"Lisa, your husband held up your new book, *Lioness Arising*, tonight at his meeting. And he told us lions are the best killers, but lionesses are the best hunters."

I thought, well, of course he would say that. It is all he knows because that's what I told him . . . he hasn't read the book yet, I'm sure! The man continued, "Well, he is right. It is true lionesses are the best hunters."

I was not sure where this conversation was going. Why was this man calling me to tell me what my husband said, which I already knew because I had written it? Well, I was about to find out.

"Lisa, do you know we are not winning the war in Afghanistan?"

I mumbled some form of acknowledgment. Living in Colorado Springs meant flying home with many service men returning from active duty.

"Do you want to know one of the reasons why we are not winning the war?"

"Sure," I volunteered.

"We can't speak to their women." He went on to explain, "If you can't speak to the women, you can't flip the culture, and if you can't flip the culture, you can't win the war."

Now he had my attention.

"Let me explain what I do here at this base. I work with special operatives. Because of the dangers involved we have focused primarily on special ops teams of men, but now we are also sending in teams of women. They will tell the Afghan women they have voice and value. They will explain why democracy will serve their sons and daughters well. They will take care of their minor medical needs and deliver their babies. Do you know what the name of this group of special ops women is?"

I assured him I did not.

He said, "They are called *Team Lioness*, and they are about to be deployed. May I have a copy of your book for all of them?"

Of course we sent them!

These women deserved to be supported as they reached out to women and nurtured the hope of something more than war and famine for their children. These lionesses needed to know they were not simply following military orders but that they were part of something more eternal, the mandate to bring healing and life to their sisters who were isolated and often despised simply because of their gender. The military men were forbidden to speak to the Afghan women, but the military women were ordered to.

After I hung up the phone, I realized once again that without the involvement of women, there are many battles that cannot be won.

If the United States military understands that without the involvement of women a nation can fight but it will not win, then isn't it high time the church empowers its daughters to come alongside the men so there is no longer just a fight but a win?

Gender rivalry has been known to swing both ways, but more often than not women are on the receiving end of the discrimination. For more than three decades I have carried in my heart the women who've been wounded in the rivalry of the sexes. I cannot author a book without addressing this issue on some level.

> **Without the involvement of women, there are many battles that cannot be won.**

Great advances have been made and on many fronts, but every week I hear the story of a woman who has suffered in her marriage, family, workplace, or house of worship. I regularly read hateful comments directed at women on social media. This does not even begin to address the issues of sex trafficking, gendercide, and pornography.

Sadly, gender prejudice still blurs the lines of our gospel; we seem to use it to extend full redemption and freedom to men while measuring controlled portions to women.

The Threats of Religious Leaders

I want to open up this topic of gender prejudice by stepping back to a time when the church was newborn, alive and growing after the resurrection, and there was an outpouring of God's Spirit on both sons and daughters. The gospel was being released in both word and deed as the resurrection of Jesus was proclaimed. Panicked temple leaders, in an attempt to calm the storm, arrested Peter and John when a man who had been lame for forty years was healed.

> They called them back and warned them that they were *on no account ever again to speak or teach in the name of Jesus.* (Acts 4:18 Message)

The *they* in this interaction refers to the religious leaders of their day, and Peter and John are the ones who were sternly warned. This wonder performed in the name of Jesus, the healing of a man, had thrown wide open a door to preach Christ the risen Savior. The Jewish leaders found themselves between a rock and a hard place because there was no denying the healing of this crippled man. They reasoned among themselves:

> By now it's known all over town that a miracle has occurred, and that they are behind it. There is no way we can refute that. But so that it doesn't go any further, *let's silence them with threats* so they won't dare to use Jesus's name ever again with anyone. (Acts 4:16–17 Message)

We all know that threatening these two disciples did not work. If anything their tactics had the very opposite effect and actually strengthened their resolve.

> But Peter and John spoke right back, "Whether it's right in God's eyes to listen to you rather than to God, you decide. As for us, there's no question—we can't keep quiet about what we've seen and heard." (Acts 4:18–20 Message)

As far as Peter and John were concerned, the religious leaders could continue to argue among themselves for as long as they liked, but they would not be stopped. They realized trying to convince these leaders would be an exercise in futility. They had no choice but to continue teaching and preaching what they knew to be true. These men understood that there are times when silence equates to disobedience.

These threats echo in our ears even today. The recipients of this threat look different now. This is no longer an isolated directive given by religious leaders to uneducated fishermen from Galilee. It has grown into a cultural push the world over. It sounds different now, but the objective is the same. Our secular world will allow you to talk about God and be as spiritual as you like, just as long as you don't use the name of Jesus.

And though we should not be surprised when secular arenas block teaching and preaching in the name of Jesus, when the church obstructs its members and silences their voices . . . well, that is another animal entirely.

For more than two millennia religious leaders have limited and at times prohibited thousands of the church's daughters from preaching and teaching in the sacred spaces under its governance. Read Acts 4:18 again:

> So they called them and charged them not to speak or teach at all in the name of Jesus.

As I pondered this verse, I heard the Holy Spirit whisper, *Far too many of the daughters I called and gifted by my Spirit for ministry have been held back and denied their call by the church.*

You might have heard religious leaders say, "Women can *teach* other women but not men." Or, "Women can *share*, but there is to be no preaching." And: "Women can lead, as long as it is outside the church." These veiled threats appear to be more reasonable, but the result is the same: the gospel is contained. Women who are bold with their faith are too quickly labeled aggressive. Women who are confident in their God are mistaken for ambitious. Yet the question before us is the same one raised by Peter and John. Is it right in the sight of God to listen to men rather than to obey God? And what has God instructed both his sons and daughters to do? We find our answer in the words Jesus spoke right before he ascended:

> "Go into all the world and proclaim the gospel to the whole creation. Whoever believes and is baptized will be saved, but whoever does not believe will be condemned. And these signs will accompany those who believe: in my name they will cast out demons; they will speak in new tongues; they will pick up serpents with their hands; and if they drink any deadly poison, it will not hurt them; they will lay their hands on the sick, and they will recover." So then the Lord Jesus, after he had spoken to them, was taken up into heaven and sat down at the right hand of God. (Mark 16:15–19)

This directive was given to *all* who believe. The Great Commission is permission, it doesn't even require a building or an organization, and this mandate is inclusive of both genders. In Christ all are called and liberated to declare God's good news. Once we've known God's freedom and truth we should never allow human threats to silence us.

Obey Your King

God is our high and holy King. Our King has commissioned and empowered you. He has asked you to speak to his people on his behalf. This being true, how could you ever allow those who lead under the King to deter you? Each of us must be a living, breathing declaration of Matthew 4:10:

> We will worship the Lord our God and serve only him.

If obeying the King's subjects means disobeying the King, then your real problem is with the King. We have an example of how to navigate this in Esther. The king of Persia had not called for Esther, and the statutes of his court forbid her to come before him. But Esther understood that obeying the king's parameters meant disobeying God. Esther feared God more than she feared the displeasure of people, and she went. She approached the king strategically, but she did not dare remain silent when so many lives were at stake. I have to wonder how different our world is today. Many daughters are hidden away in strategic places and circumstances. Some are even now fasting and praying alongside their sisters, watching and waiting for the right moment to step in and intercede.

Having said this, I am not endorsing rebellion to your husband or to church leaders. I am hoping to heighten your awareness that there is a very real enemy who will not be content with simply silencing you. He is after your life and the lives of your children.

Truth time. If your husband forbade you from sharing the gospel, would you obey him?

I'm not talking about ascending the pulpit in the role of senior pastor or speaking publicly. I am asking, are you sincerely free and able to be a witness? Are you ready to give an answer, to pray, or to disciple a younger woman?

John and I were talking about this issue recently. He asked me why so many women seem to be looking for excuses to opt out of being an ambassador for Jesus. I shared that I believe some are simply afraid of the backlash. It was the same week I sat next to a man on a plane who shared with me that I was called a derogatory term behind my back. I answered, "And to my face as well!"

This is not the time for the faint of heart or the thin of skin. It is all-out war against the image bearers of God, both male and female. The last thing we need to be caught doing is fighting amongst one another! Having said this, I do think some women need to brave this conversation. They may have been taught that submission is silence, and they do not know that God has changed their names. What is God prompting you to do? Is there a young mother who needs you to disciple her? What about hosting a prayer group or Bible study in your home? Godly submission honors our husbands while obeying God.

Other women are afraid of their strengths because no one has ever taught them how to steward them. We have all seen or been women behaving poorly. (I know I've mishandled things.) It wasn't because I wanted to be difficult but because I didn't know how to make myself heard. The learning curve is steep because until recently the women in this world have been few and far between.

The answer is not the elimination of the feminine voice; it is the education of women. If I am not allowed the opportunity for growth, I will not grow. If I do not grow, I do not make room for others.

Are we going to allow ourselves to be labeled angry women? Or will we gain wisdom so the daughters with their Father's Word in their mouths can speak? Should those with a portion of the answer be silenced? God forbid! We should actively be training up our daughters in godliness and obedience. And for those who ask how this is in keeping with 1 Peter 3, which outlines that women are to be meek and of a quiet spirit—I absolutely agree! And I have examples of how to be meek in the lives of Jesus and Moses.

> Now the man Moses was very meek, more than all people who were on the face of the earth. (Num. 12:3)

And,

> Take my yoke upon you, and learn from me, for I am gentle and lowly in heart [*meek*], and you will find rest for your souls. (Matt. 11:29)

Both Jesus and Moses modeled meekness as an example for us to follow.

Some of our issues with gender are just silly. I don't ask John if I can have friends over, and he doesn't ask me if he can go golfing. I don't ask John if I can share Jesus with someone at Target or if I can preach to the youth at our home church. We consult each other on things that affect both of us and our family but not on how we steward our days. If we went to each other for every little thing, it would be exhausting—and he trusts me and I trust him! I am a wife, not a child.

We live in a day and time when far too many people are captive to fear. They need the hope of glory that you carry in your heart.

Ultimately, we alone are to blame for our disobedience to Jesus's commission. Yes, others can cause us to stumble and sin (Matt. 18:6; Mark 9:42; Luke 17:2), but obedience to our King is ultimately our choice. Just like our brothers Peter and John, we sisters must walk in the fullness of the wonder of Christ, and this means we likewise can't keep quiet about what we've seen and heard.

Verbal Attacks

In our time, the women who choose this course might not be beaten or imprisoned as Peter and John were, but prepare to be shunned and resisted. This means you will run the risk of being misinterpreted, and very often you will suffer verbal attacks and isolation.

John and I have different vantage points on this dynamic. He assured me that most of the churches he goes to receive women into their pulpits. He went on to name three women ministers, all of whom are well known and loved in our nation and beyond. They lead, teach, *and* preach. I agreed with John that in theory this was true, but not in practice. When I asked him to name churches that regularly welcome women to the pulpit, and once a year on Mother's Day doesn't count, he came up with less than ten.

As our discussion continued, John assured me there was nothing I could say, as a woman, that would ever change the mind of the theologians who oppose women in leadership and teaching capacities. He suggested I use my words to teach and tell the women they can preach. That any argument I proposed would be wasted on the leaders.

I agreed; leaders are not my focus. I write with fear and trembling to my sisters and the mothers and daughters who yet need convincing. I explained that I cannot teach women to *preach* when they are still unsure whether it is right for them to *teach* and *speak* in the church. The letter of the law has been used to pierce their hearts. No sincere daughter of God wants to violate or desecrate her Father's will. They will not learn what the leaders do not allow. If someone who is an authority figure who represents God tells you all your life that you are *inferior*, you will believe it. This lie is especially easy to receive if you have a shadowed past.

I *know* this because I have *been* this.

When you are unsure, you will constantly second-guess yourself and your right to contribute. I want to unplug your ears and remove the blinders from your eyes and remove the thorn of legalism from your tender hearts. Then you can heal and hear for yourself. The Holy Spirit may call you to be an ambassador of the gospel in the realm of law, medicine, business, government, or as a stay-at-home mother. Anything and everything we do should be as unto the Lord. This practice makes the secular sacred. But it is wrong to tell someone that the Holy Spirit is not speaking to them if they feel called to teach, preach, or lead in some capacity in the church.

Gender has little to do with someone's capacity to lead. The fact that Margaret Thatcher was a woman was not what ultimately qualified her to be one of the United Kingdom's greatest leaders. Actually, gender is not the problem; our challenge is a posture of pride and a tendency toward prejudice and judging others. These will blind someone who is otherwise a good leader. Humility, experience, faithfulness, education, and virtue are just some of the qualities that qualify leaders, but gender alone does not a leader make. And apart from Christ we are all unfit. We read in 2 Corinthians 3:4–6:

> Such is the confidence that we have through Christ toward God. Not that we are sufficient in ourselves to claim anything as coming from us, but our sufficiency is from God, who has made us sufficient to be ministers of a new covenant, not of the letter but of the Spirit. For the letter kills, but the Spirit gives life.

And yet here is how one prominent leader interpreted 1 Timothy 2: "Paul is simply stating that when it comes to leading in the church, women are unfit because they are more gullible and easier to deceive than men."[1]

We'll get to the Scripture in Timothy in a moment. First, I must know: How did this quote make you feel? Shamed, guilty, violated? Relieved and excused?

It certainly can't make any of us feel empowered and included. I almost didn't include the quote, but it captures a mind-set behind the widespread censure of women. This leader went on to say, "While many irate women have disagreed with his [Paul's] assessment through the years, it does appear from this that such women who fail to trust his instruction and follow his teaching are much like their mother Eve and are well-intended but ill-informed."[2]

Do we have to be irate to disagree? I disagree with my husband without becoming irate. My staff and I disagree without becoming irate, and so do my friends and I.

The assumption is if we disagree with this assessment of 1 Timothy 2, it is because we are irate, ill-informed women. No allowance is given that we might be godly, thinking, inquisitive women trying to navigate gender as we seek to obey God. It doesn't even offer the possibility that Paul might be addressing something that was present in his culture and absent in ours.

This explanation also gives us the wrong source of identity. Eve is not our mother. Once we are born again we are no longer the children of our fallen parents, Adam and Eve. We become children of God.

In this author's words I hear a desire to silence and shame. I hear sexist bullying and misogyny. What I don't hear is the Holy Spirit. When Jesus teaches and instructs, it is with love and acceptance of all. He likened his church to a bride. The words of this author are more in keeping with the serpent's enmity toward women.

First Timothy was written by Paul to address issues Timothy was facing in pioneering a church in a Greek culture. Does what applied to them apply to us today, when absolutely nothing is the same in our worship services or culture? Maybe you are yet unsure. Perhaps because you want to honor God and never question leadership, you've accepted this designation as your lot in life.

Let's probe a bit further. Would you allow your daughter to be spoken to with these words? Would you stand by in silent agreement while someone called her unfit, gullible, easy to deceive, or ill-informed? Would this ever be a life-giving, Spirit-breathed way to correct or describe anyone, male or female? Have you ever imagined, even for a moment, that God the Father looks at any area of your life and labels you permanently with these fallen traits?

I understand you may have spoken these very words over yourself. If you have been a Christian for a while, there may have been a time or times when a teacher or leader spoke these same ideas over the lives of the women in your church. Just recently a woman who has ministered for years called our organization and questioned if what she was doing was scriptural because of all the persecution she was under.

This I can promise you, my daughter, my sister, my friend: our bridegroom and Lord, Jesus, has never spoken these diminishing words over you. He has never once told me I dishonored him by the act of preaching. That does not mean I can't improve—I self-assess after every service. Believe me, I feel the Spirit's correction in every realm of my life. But when it comes to doing what he has called me to do and how he sees me, there is a perpetual whisper of encouragement. Listen to what he says of you and me: he calls you altogether lovely, fit, and well able. He has given you a new heart and a quickened spirit that makes you wise and true. He has filled you with the Holy Spirit and entrusted you with the Word of God so that rather than a deceived daughter, the eyes of your understanding will be enlightened with discernment (Ps. 45:11; Ezek. 36:26; 2 Cor. 3:6; Eph. 1:18).

His bride is made up of male and female. He has washed all of us of our filth with the water of his Word and in the process redeemed both genders by his blood. And yet when I read that particular interpretation of 1 Timothy 2 to the women who gathered regularly in my home for Bible study, I saw resignation in their faces, along with shock and horror. There were those who thought what he had to say had an element of truth; perhaps they had been gullible or unfit in their past. Others had given up thinking it would ever be interpreted differently.

When I asked you about your daughters, did something stir inside you? I hope something fierce and maternal rose up within you. And what about you? Are you okay with limits for yourself rather than the freedom Christ purchased? If you wouldn't allow limits for your daughter, you shouldn't allow them for yourself. In Ephesians 2:10 we are told, "For we are his workmanship, created in Christ Jesus for good works, which God prepared beforehand, that we should walk in them."

I hope and pray you will never resign yourself to a designation of unfit, gullible, and easy to deceive. If we are ill-informed we can change that by becoming educated and well-informed. I decided to take that as a challenge to myself, gathering resources from people smarter than me. First, let's look at Paul's directives in light of each other. In 1 Corinthians 14:34–35 we read:

> Wives must not disrupt worship, talking when they should be listening, asking questions that could more appropriately be asked of their husbands at home. God's Book of the law guides our manners and customs here. Wives have no license to use the time of worship for unwarranted speaking. (Message)

And then in 1 Timothy 2:11–15:

> I don't let women take over and tell the men what to do. They should study to be quiet and obedient along with everyone else. Adam was made first, then Eve: woman was deceived first—our pioneer in sin!—with Adam right on her heels. On the other hand, her childbearing brought about salvation, reversing Eve. But this salvation only comes to those who

continue in faith, love, and holiness, gathering it all into maturity. You can depend on this. (Message)

The entire gathering of Greeks would have been learning about Christianity together. Women were no longer to assume the position they had among pagans: the position of oracles that the temple worship of Diana had given them. When we read Paul's instruction to Timothy about church order, he was not quoting the law. He was not quoting Jesus. He was making suggestions to Timothy on how to decently gather new believers in Greek culture. At the time, in their culture, women were seen as the authorities on spiritual matters.[3]

In The Passion Translation, which is taken from the Aramaic, Paul's words in 1 Timothy 2:11–12 read:

> Let the women who are new converts be willing to learn with all submission to their leaders and not speak out of turn. I don't advocate that the newly converted women be teachers in the church, assuming authority over the men, but to live in peace. For God formed Adam first, then Eve. Adam did not mislead Eve, but Eve misled him and violated the command of God. Yet a woman shall live in restored dignity by means of her children, receiving the blessing that comes from raising them as consecrated children nurtured in faith and love, walking in wisdom.

To find answers on how this translates to modern-day practice, I turned to a theologian and church leader who has worked practically with the dynamic of women preaching and leading in a thriving local church. Dr. Gilbert Bilezikian, a Wheaton college professor and Willow Creek Church elder, spearheaded an eighteen-month study on the issues of women in leadership. Here are some of his findings, first reported in his book *Beyond Sex Roles*:

> In summary, we concluded that before the Fall, men and women related to each other as co-regents, both bearing the image of God and called to join together in caring for the world he had created. Both men and women are responsible to fulfill their ministries of service for God's glory in the manner God had gifted them and to the degree to which they had apportioned faith. Tragically, in the Fall, this cooperative relationship was deeply wounded. We believe God's gracious plan for redemption is that everything that was broken through sin—including the relationship between men and women—might be restored to the beauty that existed during the first days of Creation. Many devout, intelligent Christians disagree with our conclusions. There will come a day when we will all find out the degree to which we have veered from God's perfect wisdom, in this issue and many others. Until then, I hold this position humbly, yet firmly. I am willing to take the risk of encouraging women to do what I believe Scriptures ask of them—to make themselves fully available to the full range of spiritual gifts.[4]

If a woman feels called to preach, teach, or lead and she lives a life qualified by the virtues outlined in Scripture, then educate her and let her receive training so she can preach, teach, and lead in whatever capacity God commissions. Along with Dr. Bilezikian, I hold this position humbly, yet firmly.

A Rabbi's Insights on Eve

Not long ago I had the privilege of speaking at length with a brilliant messianic rabbi, Brian Bileci. I shared with him my concern that far too many of God's daughters have no idea who they are. It is becoming increasingly obvious that the identity and dignity of God's daughters are under vicious assault by the spirit of this world, and far too many houses of worship do not know how to foster the gifts God has given to women.

Male and female were created to be separate in expression but never to be divided in purpose.

I wanted to know from a lifelong Hebrew scholar what God thought of his daughters. I asked him to begin with Eve and then continue through Sarah and forward all the way to Christ's bride, the Church. The rabbi told me many things, and here are a few nuggets I wanted to pass on to you, because they will help you affirm your identity.

God did not love Adam more and Eve less. From the beginning Eve was always within Adam. Though Adam named her and even needed her, Eve was always God's idea. God gave Eve her unique feminine perspective and expression. The woman was always within the man, which is why the man does better with her than without her (Gen. 2:18). The introduction of Eve changed Adam's "not good" to "so very good."

We know from the Scriptures that Adam was put into a deep sleep and his side was opened up and Eve was formed (Gen. 2:21). Male and female were uniquely separated, but each is not a disjointed half. They are two complete wholes. Male and female were created to be separate in expression but never to be divided in purpose. It is important to note that there were no role divisions before the fall. Therefore, the two could be one in purpose, one in heart, and one in physical union.

One tragic day Eve was deceived and Adam rebelled. Eve's choice did not predestine *all* women with an unregenerate propensity toward deception any more than Adam's betrayal predisposed *all* men toward rebellion. Too frequently I hear attempts to paint Adam's sin as though it was somehow a *lesser evil* than Eve's. I have heard it referred to as just a "sin of omission." The rabbi disagreed. He confirmed what the Scriptures teach:

> For as by one man's disobedience the many were made sinners, so by one man's obedience the many will be made righteous. (Rom. 5:19)

Adam's sin was not omission. At its best it might be labeled "willful disobedience," but some scholars would call it traitorous rebellion.

I have to wonder if Adam and Eve didn't also attempt a kind of identity theft: after all, they wanted to be God!

In our house, when our children willfully ignore parental instruction and listen to the voices of friends or even each other, we do not call their actions omission. We call their choice disobedience. In military terms, if a command is willfully disobeyed, it is called insubordination, not omission. And now read God's description of Adam's transgression:

> Because you have listened to the voice of your wife and have eaten of the tree of which I commanded you, "You shall not eat of it," cursed is the ground because of you. (Gen. 3:17)

For some reason a trend that downplays Adam's role has arisen. (I am not sure why any feel the need to defend Adam's choices or actions since all of us are now redeemed in Christ.)

These adherents charge the men to rise up and be good leaders, an admonishment to which I add my hearty "yes and amen." I agree there is a desperate need for those who would model examples for males. My concern is aroused by how some advocate this process. They believe the men of the church would lead best by silencing the voices of women, gaining their reasoning by going all the way back to the fall.

I find many flaws in this reasoning and approach. There is little doubt that much harm could have been averted if Adam had stepped in and spoken truth. His foresight and attention to God's directive would have been best used on the serpent/deceiver, however, rather than on Eve. Adam should have used his voice to silence the serpent; after all, we do not wrestle with flesh and blood. Likewise, men should now use their voices to silence evil—not women whom God created in his own image and called good.

The best way to protect someone from making future mistakes is open instruction, not prohibition. The fact that Eve made a grave mistake in her past should not silence her daughters' voices in the future, as surely as Adam's sin should not bind his sons! For more than twenty centuries men and women have been learning side by side in the church. It is time we realize who we are in Christ and lead side by side just as we were originally created to function in the garden. Men leading as men and women leading as women.

Now we have the model of Jesus, who showed us the right pattern for interactions with Satan:

> Be gone, Satan! For it is written, "You shall worship the Lord your God and him only shall you serve." (Matt. 4:10)

We are to echo God's words rather than become mired down in a reasoning match. Let's serve God so stunningly that we are living, breathing arguments for living a life of faith. And our ultimate example is Jesus. We are to walk as he walked. We are to follow him even more than we follow anyone, including Paul. Paul himself counseled Timothy to follow Paul only in the ways and according to the patterns that he followed Christ: "Be imitators of me, as I am of Christ" (1 Cor. 11:1).

Satan's Lies; God's Healing

Satan robs both men and women when we listen to his divisive counsel and add strength to one gender by subtracting it from the other. Time is slipping away. It is time we follow the mandate of Jesus and continue to seek to save that which was lost (Luke 19:10). It is far past time for the church to be a living, breathing example to a broken, segregated world of a way to live that is multiracial, multigenerational, and unites the genders in purpose. By mishandling issues of gender we have left both genders fragmented and wounded. When we recover our God identity, the healing of gender will begin.

Sometimes the confusion is so great that women question their own gender identity, feeling they should have been born a man. Many are attempting to heal themselves by changing their gender or embracing androgyny. Read the words of God through the prophet Isaiah:

> You turn things upside down! Shall the potter be regarded as the clay, that the thing made should say of its maker, "He did

not make me"; or the thing formed say of him who formed it, "He has no understanding"? (Isa. 29:16)

The question remains, do we trust God? Do we believe he is good and wise and did not make a mistake when he fashioned us in our mothers' wombs as daughters? Can he ultimately have a purpose in our disappointment that taking matters into our own hands circumvents?

Believe me, I understand the wounding. I also realize that for many the pain goes far deeper than I have known . . . and yet God can reach in and touch what human hands can never heal. I distinctly remember resenting the fact that I was a woman. I don't know if it was due to the volatile relationship I had with my mother or just a preemptive attack of the enemy to undermine the plan of God on my life. Whether it was because of incidents in my life, relationships with women, or encounters in the church, the truth was I disliked the vulnerabilities associated with womanhood. I was a tomboy growing up and had more male friends than female friends. I liked guys better. When puberty hit, I felt like an alien forced into a world of pink and beauty. Girls spoke a language of hints and whispers that I didn't understand, and they moved with a grace and beauty this gangly girl did not possess. Throughout high school I dressed in jeans and overalls in large part to cover my lack of feminine shape and to hide my painful self-consciousness.

When John and I got engaged, I tried to carefully explain to him that I was a woman's body with a man's brain. (John immediately told me this was not an option!) On the positive side, I truly believe a lot of it was God's way of preparing me for life with four sons! God took me on a healing journey.

He whispered intimate value into my womanhood. In his presence, all the shame that religion had coated the image of women with was replaced with garments of splendor. He reached deep into my soul and gave me courage and strength in place of the fear and victim mentality my mother had unconsciously attached to my femininity. I learned to love my body not merely for what it looked like but also for what it could do. It was a process and a journey that I have been able to share so that others too have found healing.

But what if I found myself struggling with my femininity in this day and age when gender reassignment is encouraged and even applauded? Our culture would have told me to take matters into my own hands and actually become a man! But by doing so I would have averted God's healing process and all the lessons I learned along the way. When we stop comparing ourselves to one another, then we are positioned to accept ourselves with all of our flaws.

So what steps can you take to see the healing begin?

1. *Pray.* Ask the Holy Spirit to give you an undivided heart and reveal any wrong thinking or areas of disobedience. Gender prejudice and resentment can creep in and taint our perspective of ourselves and one another. Pray to be a minister of reconciliation, not of division.

2. *Submit your will to God.* Perhaps you have held back or hidden behind the rules of man rather than obey what you have known and seen in the Scriptures and what's been revealed to you in prayer. Maybe you have allowed the fear of man (or the fear of being a woman) to keep you back from the will of God. Ask God how the Great Commission should look in your life and in

this season with the understanding that it may look different in the next season.

3. *Know your enemy*. We are not wrestling with flesh and blood. And when we are double minded, we behave like double agents. James tells us that once we have submitted to God we are to resist the devil and he must flee.

4. *Examine your life and conversations*. What are you saying and doing that might be feeding gender prejudice? If the Holy Spirit revealed areas of your life that have been compromised, then it is very likely these prejudices or resentments have been communicated.

5. *Take a stand*. People who do not stand for anything run the risk of falling for everything. Those who oppose women and men working together have unintentionally set themselves at odds with God's original mandate.

6. *Fight for unity in the body of Christ*. Men and women are not rivals. We are brothers and sisters, guardians and intimate allies. We are to walk together with the fellowship, mutual respect, and affection of brothers and sisters. And we are to encourage the gifts of each other. God would never have granted women a voice if he intended for them to remain silent. God knew that Adam, and our world, would need the voice and influence of women.

Complementary and Interdependent

I want my granddaughters empowered to think, study, and ask questions so they can truly learn and by learning live out their faith. We say women can be born again, but there are yet doctrines and dogma in place that deny that they have been truly and completely set free. It would be more accurate to say that most women are free to operate within the confines of the church rather than within the commission of Christ.

Unwise men and women have resorted to blaming one another for their bad choices since the garden. Blaming and shaming have never truly helped anyone move forward. Blame and shame muddy the water and cloud the image of both the sons and the daughters. This tack makes what God made clean in Christ appear dirty and obscene once again.

Gender was created to express divine beauty. Sadly, we have stripped one another of our divine dignity and strength in an attempt to get from one another the approval and affirmation only God can ultimately give us. God created us to celebrate one another's differences, not to demean or disrespect them.

And now in Christ our nakedness is clothed in righteousness. In Christ male and female remember they are allies, not enemies. Paul's words in 1 Corinthians 11:10–12 give us a better look at what we can and should be for each other. Let's expound upon this passage verse by verse. The Message paraphrase of verse 10 reads:

> Don't, by the way, read too much into the differences here between men and women. Neither man nor woman can go it alone or claim priority.

In Christ men and women are interdependent rather than independent. Our source is ultimately God, but these verses address the age-old rivalry known as the battle of the sexes.

Our differences were meant to complement one another. Where there is mutual dependence and inclusion, supremacy and hierarchy are eliminated. The poetic words of The Message continue to dismantle this rivalry this way:

> Man was created first, as a beautiful shining reflection of God—that is true. But the head on a woman's body clearly outshines in beauty the head of her "head," her husband. (v. 11)

Here Paul switches from male and female to more specifically man and wife. I love the value this bestows on both genders. My husband makes me look good by the way he loves God, me, and our children, just as I want to make him look good by the way I love God, our family, and him. Then Paul returns to the more general topic of gender rather than the dynamic of marriage.

> The first woman came from man, true—but ever since then, every man comes from a woman! (v. 12)

Woman's origin was woven within the side of a man, and now man is woven inside the womb of a woman. Woman was the first born of a man, Adam, and then we are all reborn from the second Adam, Jesus. Paul goes on:

> And since virtually everything comes from God anyway, let's quit going through these "who's first" routines. (v. 12)

The rivalry of who is first and who is best should come to a screeching halt with the revelation of who God is. We need to recover our divine perspective that God alone is holy. He is first and last, the beginning and the end, our Alpha and our Omega. No one leads or loves like our Father.

This means he does not love sons more and daughters less. Nor does he love each gender equally. He loves male and female uniquely. When we elevate one above the other, we deviate from his image because God chose gender as an expression of himself.

Men and Women in the Early Church

Without a healthy understanding of our history we often diminish our destiny, but I have no doubt that the Holy Spirit is tearing away the veil the enemy has sought to place over our understanding. When we review the Scriptures, there is no escaping the fact that the early church was a force to be reckoned with. When their culture tried to restrict their movement it only served to cause them to expand and take new territory. They did not cower under the orders of earthly kings because they had already bowed their knee to the God Most High. They walked *daily* in signs, wonders, and miracles. They lived with the understanding that their ultimate authority was found in the realm unseen.

They were marked by God's Spirit, set apart for exploits. Do not imagine it was the men on one side and the women on the other in their sanctuaries; more often than not they met in homes, in the marketplace, in secret gatherings in the catacombs, and even on ships and in prisons. These believers hailed from every tribe, tongue, and custom and yet were united by one and the same Holy Spirit; both genders stood together to form one body, the bride of Christ. When we are one, there is no side but God's. They shared the gospel from house to house. We see a window of how this body organically grew in Acts 2:42–44:

And they devoted themselves to the apostles' teaching and the fellowship, to the breaking of bread and the prayers. And awe came upon every soul, and many wonders and signs were being done through the apostles. And all who believed were together and had all things in common.

This phrase "all things in common" should not be limited to their needs; it included their worship, awe, fellowship, meals, prayers, and possessions. *Common* means mutual, widespread, everyday, and communal.

Men and women were close enough to be devoted to one another in the areas of both fellowship and teaching. Teaching without fellowship does not create a community that ministers to the needs of one another. If anything, teaching without discussion around the table will feed an elitist mentality or distort the truth. What we learn is tested in how we live the truth, not by what we know as truth. Far too many are held captive by the conflict of what they know in their heads that they do not live out in their lives. It takes both family and friends to keep us holistic in our posture and application of truth.

In this early church, the women had a voice. If this were not the case, then the incident with Ananias and Sapphira would have played out differently. In Acts 5:1–11, we have the story of a husband who in the absence of his wife lies to Peter and drops dead. Three hours later his wife shows up. She knows nothing about the death of her husband, but she does know what she is supposed to give as an answer. When Peter questions her, she repeats the lie that she and her husband had agreed on, and like him she also falls over dead. My point here is that under much of the submission teaching we receive today, she would have been "covering or honoring her husband's wishes" by lying. But when Sapphira chose to lie rather than tell the truth, the penalty was her life. She misused her voice. If she had spoken the truth to Peter, she would have lived.

When there is an overwhelming revelation of mercy and grace, there is no room for anyone to be left out. Women and men both had valid contributions. Many of them were experiencing this dynamic for the very first time. What the fall had taken away God had anointed them to be part of restoring. Men and women labored together in "the fields of their cities and the far flung corners of the earth" with grace and power. Acts 2:46–47 describes the rhythm of the early church this way:

> And day by day, attending the temple together and breaking bread in their homes, they received their food with glad and generous hearts, praising God and having favor with all the people. And the Lord added to their number day by day those who were being saved.

The verses paint the day-to-day rhythm that graced the early church. The Jewish believers would attend temple together, gather in homes filled with fellowship, and sit around tables with thankful, generous hearts. Their lives overflowed with the praise of their God, and they walked in favor among the people.

Why would we imagine that the bride of Jesus, his church, would ever exclude, diminish, demean, or downplay women? Why did we accept the lie that we were not likewise heroes?

For far too long the idea of *men and women together* has been hidden. The fallout of living life segregated by selfishness and prejudice has left both genders wounded.

But this is not the end of our story or the final word. In heaven's design, gender is neither an issue of wounding nor a battleground of rivalry. We are brought together by our differences, stronger together than we ever have been apart. The greatness of God's sons and daughters living as one may yet be revealed on this earth. And through our unity, the image of God will be unveiled, and the glory of God will at last shine forth in all its dazzling splendor.

Discussion Questions

1. What are some of the battles the men are having to fight on their own?
2. As a woman, have you ever experienced the tension between the call of God and the limits of the traditions of men?
3. What does the Great Commission look like in your life?
4. How did the descriptions of "unfit," "more gullible," and "easier to deceive" make you personally feel?
5. How can you increase your skill level in the way you handle the gospel?
6. In what areas have you been trapped in the blame game?

7

The Rivalry of Fear and Love

Love is the beauty of the soul.

St. Augustine

Recently, John and I did a joint question-and-answer session on marriage at one of our favorite churches. This Sunday night gathering happened among those who feel like family. As the session closed, this big question came up. "After more than thirty years of marriage, is there anything that looking back you would have done differently?" This one fell to me to answer. With time running short, I wanted to be both truthful and concise. I took a deep breath and confessed, "I would have allowed John the right to make more mistakes, and I would have loved him more fearlessly."

It was as though a ripple traveled through the crowd. From where I sat I saw men and women hurriedly wipe away tears;

there were many deep sighs and silent nods. Fear is the greatest rival of love . . . equal in intensity and deadly in its capacity to corrupt.

So many of the things I feared in our marriage never even came close to happening. The worries that tormented me at night only lined my face. They were never as much as a brushstroke on the canvas of my life. This wasn't because I had painted so well; it was because of the stunning faithfulness of God.

I don't enjoy making mistakes any more than the next person. But looking back I would have taken more risks. I will never know this side of heaven how much my fear robbed the both of us. I do know this . . . fear is an awful marriage counselor. It will paralyze and hold captive what love longs to release into motion. For whether or not we realize it, love and risk are intimately connected.

I was raised in a household where fear ruled rather than love. Fear had a constant voice in my parents' marriage. It wove itself into their friendships, even as it drained our family's finances. There was never enough money, never enough love, and never enough people to trust. Fear echoed its doom through the rooms of our beautiful house and bounced off the blank walls without pictures. My father was a builder, but fear made sure that we lived in houses that never felt like homes. Countless nights my brother and I would lie in our beds struggling to fall asleep as our parents fought late into the night. By the light of a flashlight I wrote notes in my diary and made vows in the dark. I thought these impassioned notes would protect me. I promised myself that I would *never* be vulnerable. My parents ultimately divorced—twice—and finally went their separate ways as enemies rather than as friends.

When I became a Christian, my heart found a home, but that didn't mean I knew how to behave in one. In the first decade of our marriage, I had to face off with so many of the faulty safety nets I had constructed as a child. Refusing to be vulnerable meant I did not know how to forgive or be forgiven. The ropes of these nets entangled me and nearly strangled our marriage. My husband was nothing like my father, and I was not my mother, and yet there were times of disagreement when I echoed the hurtful words I'd learned when my parents thought I was fast asleep.

I was bringing their legacy of fear into my future, and I needed to stop before it took over our home as well. John's imperfections were exposing mine on a much grander scale than I imagined possible. Rather than do what I knew to be true, I acted out the script I had learned in my childhood.

Even though I had been forgiven much, I portioned out mercy to John like a miser. Our marriage covenant was fast becoming a contract, and our love was shrinking in the process.

I refused to love John fearlessly because *I* was afraid.

In an attempt to protect myself, I began to reclaim large portions of the real estate of my heart. In the first few years of our marriage, I learned that John had brought both pornography and masturbation into our relationship. (John and I have been very open about this.) Forgetting how merciful John had been with me when it came to my past, I pulled away from him. Somehow Jesus's admonishment to forgive as we have been forgiven had disappeared with the revelation of John's sin. I lived in fear and shamed him as he struggled to get free with little or no support from me. This was not approached as *our* challenge . . . it was his. Part of the reason I did not help was because I was beginning to feel the weight of my own past bear down on me and consequently believed I didn't deserve any better than what I was experiencing.

We began to fight incessantly. I moved away emotionally and watched his struggle from a distance. On some level judging him made me feel safe. If he didn't change, I didn't have to forgive him. This caused other areas of our lives to be stressed as well. I have no doubt this made our first few years harder than they needed to be.

One night in all of my anger and brokenness I cried out to God, "I will forgive him when he changes."

As far as I was concerned, all trust was broken between John and me, and I didn't want to be disappointed yet again. God answered my declaration with a question: "Do you trust me, Lisa?"

"Yes."

"Good. I need you to forgive John so he can change."

He even gave me the words to say: "I believe you want to change and I forgive you."

This was in stark contrast to my normal script, which read, "I will believe you are sorry when you change."

This way of thinking was so far removed from anything I had known that I knew it was God leading me. When I extended this unconditional mercy to John, the healing began for both of us. He was able to move out of the darkness of shame and into the light, where he found freedom from his bondage. This shift in perspective was a turning point. I could trust the unchangeable God.

Fearless Love

Fearless love is not based on the performance of a person but on the loving faithfulness of God. When I confess my sins and struggles to the Father in Jesus's name, I am never shamed. He believes my future will be better.

It is not unusual that when people disappoint us we begin to dole out love in proportion to their infractions to minimize any future risk. Afraid of going all in . . . we hold back. C. S. Lewis wisely explained the error of this approach in his book *The Four Loves*:

> To love at all is to be vulnerable. Love anything and your heart will be wrung and possibly broken. If you want to make sure of keeping it intact you must give it to no one, not even an animal. Wrap it carefully round with hobbies and little luxuries; avoid all entanglements. Lock it up safe in the casket or coffin of your selfishness. But in that casket, safe, dark, motionless, airless, it will change. It will not be broken; it will become unbreakable, impenetrable, irredeemable. To love is to be vulnerable.[1]

There you have it. *To love is to be vulnerable.* We may not like this pairing, but I have learned there is simply no way to avoid this. (And believe me, I've tried.) But don't assume that *vulnerable* means you are positioned to be *violated*. Actually, it is more likely that you are positioning yourself to be *vindicated*, because love never fails.

Let's delve a bit deeper into the risk of vulnerability. One of the definitions of *vulnerable* is "exposed." *Vulnerable* could easily be equated with *naked*. Getting naked is risky because there is nothing hidden and nothing protected.

Love is ideally a place of safety where you are naked and unashamed.

Our culture makes the leap from naked to sexual far too fast. I want to position this as naked and unafraid with a heart laid bare. We are in the strongest position when we stand openly before our God. It feels counterintuitive, but it is far better to be naked before God than to vainly cover our humanity with rags of shame or garments of self-righteousness.

Jesus became vulnerable on our behalf when he stripped himself of his divine nature to become like us so we could become like him. Jesus became vulnerable in order to reveal God's love to us. This is the reason we can love fearlessly . . . believe outrageously . . . and hope scandalously.

If you are going to love fearlessly, then go ahead and believe for the outrageous. Anchor your hopes out there in waters so deep that it is appalling.

Faith, hope, and love: these three abide. They live harmoniously intertwined with one another to give us the strength to stand. The greatest of these three forces is love. Without love there is no true act of faith, and without love there is no hope.

God is love. Love is eternal. Love never fails, and nothing entrusted to love is ever lost, and everything that is birthed out of love cannot die. But there are some places that love does not grow; love cannot flourish in the company of its rival, fear. Fear has an end—actually, fear is a dead end. Fear is an ungodly spirit that leads to torment. Fear advises from its seat in the shadow of doubt, while love draws its wisdom from the light of faith. If you heed the counsel of fear for too long or too well . . . you will fail.

Many years ago when I was writing my first book, I had a revelation that the opposite of fear is not faith or even courage . . . it is love. I should have remembered the lessons of my childhood that it was love that made the Cowardly Lion in *The Wizard of Oz* courageous. This idea really unfolded when I inserted the opposing attributes of fear into 1 Corinthians 13:

The opposite of fear is not faith or even courage . . . it is love.

> Fear is impatient and unkind while it envies and boasts; it is arrogant and rude. Fear insists on its own way; it is irritable and resentful; rejoices at wrongdoing, rather than in truth. Fear bears nothing, believes nothing, hopes nothing, endures nothing. Fear will end.

The fruit and motivations of fear are in opposition to the ways of love. Anything good that I have ever done, any life lesson I have ever learned, was realized when I moved beyond the veil of fear.

There are thrill seekers who love the rush of danger. They are brave, but only those who love are fearless.

God is love. Love is fearless. God is fearless. We are God's. We can love fearlessly. We are positioned to love fearlessly when we receive God's fearless love for us. Those who love fearlessly . . . live fearlessly.

Perhaps this progression seems obvious, and yet there are many who behave as if God has been caught off guard. We are frightened or angered by what we hear and see, and we imagine that his response to cruelty, wickedness, and calamity would mirror ours. But it doesn't.

Perfect Love

Without the motive of love the courageous just flaunt their bravado. Their acts are motivated more to impress others than to exemplify their love. *Appearing* brave is not enough, for the most courageous thing anyone can do is put themselves in harm's way on behalf of another. This means there are times when we lay our lives down rather than rise up in battle.

> Greater love has no one than this, that someone lay down his life for his friends. (John 15:13)

The Message says,

> This is the very best way to love. Put your life on the line for your friends.

This act isn't for show . . . it is for friends. First Corinthians 13:3 weighs courage and sacrifice without love thus:

> If I give away all I have, and if I deliver up my body to be burned, but have not love, I gain nothing.

A vow of poverty or an act of martyrdom *without love* is nothing more than a religious sacrifice.

Jesus was loved deeply by his Father, and he chose to love us just as deeply as the Father loved him. Love gave him the strength to endure in faith, and we are his vision of hope.

Jesus loved me in spite of my past. He was not afraid that I would make a mistake in my future. He knew I would. Even though we all *make mistakes*, that does not mean you are *a mistake*. If you think you are a mistake . . . then you are mistaken.

Even though I sin, it doesn't mean I am a sin. No matter how I feel about it, Jesus has made me righteous. The most fearless, loving response I can have to his hopes for me is to honor his faith with an obedient life.

> For our sake *he made him to be sin* who knew no sin, so that in him we might become the righteousness of God. (2 Cor. 5:21)

Jesus promised to be the answer that far outweighs any of our problems. You can spend all your time and energy focused on your sin and it won't be long until that is all you can see. You will be overwhelmed by your sinfulness, and when it becomes too much, you will turn your gaze to the sinfulness of others. I am never surprised when I learn that a leader who is hard on other people is the hardest on themselves. When I look at myself, I see flaws; when I look to Christ, my imperfections are lost in his radiance. I like the view he gives me so much better.

> Those who look to him are radiant, and their faces shall never be ashamed. (Ps. 34:5)

Jesus does not allow our sins and shadows to shroud his love. When we feel vulnerable, it is the perfect time to lift our gaze in hope rather than avert our eyes in shame. His perfect love opposes all our fears. Why would I allow my imperfect fears to oppose his flawless love? Even if I don't understand the "why" in this equation, I have learned I can trust the "who" that is in it. Because God's love is without rival. He set his love on me; therefore I choose to set my hope on him. Permit me a few alterations to Psalm 91 so we can see God's message for his women.

Because she holds fast to me in love, I will deliver her; I will protect her, because she knows my name. (v. 14)

When you really think about it . . . how can love put us at risk when love cannot fail? Love has the power to heal whatever life wounds.

There are many ways to love fearlessly.

Boldly loving your spouse is but one area. Children and parents should be loved fearlessly. Our friendships should be nurtured with love rather than with jealousy, possessiveness, and fear. You can love what you do and where you work. You may love being part of an organization or a church. You can love reading and laughing. Regardless of where you find love, sooner or later you will likewise find challenges and even disappointment.

Which brings up the next step: loving your enemies. Why would Jesus suggest such a thing?

Because it is this kind of love that separates the sheep from the goats. We are distinguished when we love those who wish us harm. When you *choose* to love the ones who would bind and injure you . . . something shifts. Even if your circumstances don't change, you are no longer trapped; you are free.

I remember reading the story of a slave during the Civil War who made the choice to bring his wounded Confederate master to the medics rather than run away and abandon him on the field of battle. It was not an easy choice, but his decision revealed that he was already truly free. This act liberated the man long before the Union army defeated the rebels.

Someone can declare freedom over you all the days of your life and you can choose to remain bound, or you can choose to walk in freedom while people foolishly imagine they own you. I understand technical slavery may never become a reality in your life, yet when people feel you owe them something it is a form of indebtedness. There are those who look free and yet live bound. You cannot control what people say about you or their perception of you, but you are able to choose your response to them.

Love chooses. Fear reacts.

Love is freedom. Fear is bondage.

Perfect love casts out fear.

Love Anyway

The following quote by Kent M. Keith is often attributed to Mother Teresa because she kept it before her as an ever-present reminder. I bet you have heard portions of it, but here it is in its entirety:

The Paradoxical Commandments

People are illogical, unreasonable, and self-centered.
Love them anyway.

If you do good, people will accuse you of selfish ulterior motives.
Do good anyway.

If you are successful, you will win false friends and true enemies.
Succeed anyway.

The good you do today will be forgotten tomorrow.
Do good anyway.

Honesty and frankness make you vulnerable.
Be honest and frank anyway.

The biggest men and women with the biggest ideas
can be shot down by the smallest men and women
with the smallest minds.
Think big anyway.

People favor underdogs but follow only top dogs.
Fight for a few underdogs anyway.

What you spend years building may be destroyed
overnight.
Build anyway.

People really need help but may attack you if you do
help them.
Help people anyway.

Give the world the best you have and you'll get
kicked in the teeth.
Give the world the best you have anyway.[2]

People will disappoint you . . . love them anyway. I find so
much of my own story of relating to others in Keith's words.
Have you ever disappointed someone? I have. They may have
shaken their heads and walked away from me muttering,
"She is such a disappointment." Enemies and even friends
will wound and betray you. You know what to do . . . love
them anyway. If you are going to build a life that is beyond
rival, then you must live beyond your human reasoning and
capacity.

I know this may not make sense at first, but when you allow
people the dignity of learning from their mistakes, you will
empower them to do better in the future.

Sadly, I feel at this point I need to put in a disclaimer. The
mistakes of which I speak do not include the following: abuse,

betrayal, or illegal actions. Mistakes fall under the categories of errors, misunderstandings, and misjudgments. These are not actions that are attached to the vile intents of perversion, cruelty, or malice. I am referring to the falls that each of us experience as we head in the right direction.

Both the righteous and the wicked trip, falter, and fall. The only difference is that love compels the righteous to get up. The wicked stay down and often attempt to pull others down alongside them, but the righteous rise up, lift others, and press on (Prov. 24:16). Love always chooses to rise again.

> Rather, *speaking the truth in love*, we are to grow up in every way into him who is the head, into Christ, from whom the whole body, joined and held together by every joint with which it is equipped, when each part is working properly, makes the body grow so that it builds itself up in love. (Eph. 4:15–16)

Speaking words of truth in love builds the body. Love causes growth in every area of life. Hateful words cause decay and retard growth. And yet love is stronger than hate and fear.

Dealing with Disappointment

Disappointment is fostered when expectations are not met. Love *believes* the best, which differs vastly from *demands* the best. Expectations can quickly translate to demands in the same manner that love will grow and translate to hope.

I trust my husband, but my ultimate hope is anchored in God. My husband and I love each other, but that doesn't mean we have not disappointed each other . . . we have. Rather than living as citizens of disappointment, we chose to leave its sad borders. We thank the incident for its input, stand up, learn what we can from our mistakes, and keep walking. We have discovered this is a better approach than choosing to continue to orbit around our disappointments as we point out each other's errors from yet another angle.

Believe me, there was a time we (or maybe it was just me!) thought this was a good idea. I thought if I examined each aspect of the mistake and surrounded each facet with enough shame then it would never happen again. (I went through this ruthless routine with both John's and my mistakes.)

This approach did not work out well because my logic was flawed. Instead, here's what happened. We became so entrenched in the pattern that all we could see were the flaws we had so astutely found in each other. We began to expect the worst of each other rather than believe the best. We both discovered in each other what we were looking for.

I love all my children, but that doesn't mean our relationships have not experienced disappointment. Though these times have been few and far between—and more often it was me who disappointed them—it's still part of our relationships. I also have friends whom I have disappointed.

Disappointment doesn't mean your love is dead; it just means it is time to schedule an appointment with the Holy Spirit and get some counsel. Love requires engagement, and real engagement requires questions and vulnerability.

Ultimately, though, I cannot expect my husband, children, or friends to be to me what only Jesus can be to me. If I do make that mistake and set them up as savior, they can't help but disappoint me because I have set them up to fall short.

Ultimately, the fault is not in their flaws but in my faulty expectations.

When you expect the best and they do less . . . you are disappointed. When you believe the best and they do less, then you understand their story is not yet over.

When you feel pressured to judge and cut off people God has called you to build with, it is a defense mechanism. Yes, there are those you walk away from because there is no agreement. Then there are those who might walk out on you. But more often than not people walk away because they don't want to be vulnerable again once they have been hurt.

God always believes better things of me than I believe of myself. He doesn't resign me to my past, because he holds my future. He draws me out of my cowardice and fear to bring out his best in me. Paul had some of these expectation struggles with the Corinthian church:

> I do admit that I have fears that when I come you'll disappoint me and I'll disappoint you, and in frustration with each other everything will fall to pieces—quarrels, jealousy, flaring tempers, taking sides, angry words, vicious rumors, swelled heads, and general bedlam. (2 Cor. 12:20 Message)

Let's stop expecting disappointment, because what we invite will come. Demanding more and withholding our approval until it happens leaves us isolated and angry, just as denying the dream leaves us hopeless. Let's believe in others what we would have them believe in us . . . that our best is yet to come. Let's believe their mistakes are but missteps. Your errors do not have the right to determine your destination.

You can respond to Jesus or you can resent your past. You alone hold that power.

We cut others off without mercy when we have not had a revelation of mercy ourselves.

The Way of Fear

Fear is costly. It will rob you blind. It will steal your strength, your dreams, your relationships, your finances, your faith, and your hope. Fear wants to taint or take away from you everything that love would freely give. Fear does not appear on the scene occasionally; its attack is as incessant as its timing is flawless.

Fear will not respect your moments of rest . . . it will invade your sleep by distorting your dreams.

Fear is a force, the spiritual antithesis of the Holy Spirit's power, love, and a sound mind. Fear comes to paralyze you just as surely as God's Spirit comes to release you.

Fear will not only rob you of so many opportunities for growth but also wants to steal your perspective of the future. Both love and fear have a plan for your life. One is for good; the other is for harm.

The Way of Love

Love, in contrast, is supremely generous. It seeks to restore your relationships, your dreams, and your hope. Every one of us has access to this way of love, promised by God. But it is a mistake to imagine that the new promises of love will stick on the old fabric of fear. God longs to pair the new with *the renewed*.

> And no one puts new wine into old wineskins. For the old skins would burst from the pressure, spilling the wine and

ruining the skins. New wine is stored in new wineskins so that both are preserved. (Matt. 9:17 NLT)

There is something *new* inside of you that fear wants to contain. Don't let it. The love of the fearless required completely new packaging. Once you have embraced the new wine of love you will begin to see everything differently. What you once saw as a chore you will now see as an opportunity to serve. You will actually seek out ways to be generous rather than pursue a life of hoarding. Love seeks to remove fear.

A Fearless Woman

Last year a close friend sent me a birthday card that I loved so much I stuck it on my mirror. The front depicts a young girl in patchwork plaid pants, and the caption reads, "It's not just the clothes, it's the attitude." In other words, it's not what you wear, it's how you wear it. Love is best worn boldly. Love is something you work.

I will tell you a compelling truth: there is nothing more attractive than a fearless woman.

Not a careless woman, a fearless one. Fearless daughters wear God's promises lit up with faith. It is only human to look *at* ourselves, and we are charged to examine ourselves in light of God's Word. But we do ourselves no favors when we look *down on* ourselves.

Fear measures us by our inability; love—fearlessly—taps into God's ability.

Fear repels, love attracts.

> There is nothing more attractive than a fearless woman.

What does it mean to be attractive?

Believe me, it is more than looks. Car wrecks attract a lot of attention. To gain a better understanding, let's go to the root word *attract*, which means "to cause to approach or adhere." It also means "to pull to or draw toward oneself as in the pull of a magnet." It also means "to excite interest and emotion."

Your life is a magnet for either curses or blessings. So ask yourself:

What is it that you are afraid of?

What is love challenging you to face?

Who is it that you refuse to forgive until they change?

Where is your love portioned out fearfully and in a measured way?

Have you woven an entangling net with declarations of fear?

It's time to turn the tables. Beginning this process is as easy as echoing heaven's declarations of unrivaled wonder over your life. So to get you started, I have fashioned a prayer for you from the words of Paul to Timothy.

My beloved daughter, I pray for a greater release of God's grace, love, and total well-being to flow into your life from God our Father and from our Lord Jesus Christ! I am writing to encourage you to fan into a flame and rekindle the fire of the spiritual gift God imparted to you. For God will never give you the spirit of cowardly fear, but the Holy Spirit gives you mighty power, love, and sound judgment!

So never be ashamed of the testimony of our Lord . . . but overcome every evil by the revelation of the power of

God. He gave us resurrection life and drew us to himself by his holy calling on our lives. And it wasn't because of any good we have done, but by his divine pleasure and marvelous grace that confirmed our union with the anointed Jesus even before time began! (2 Tim. 1:2, 6–9, adapted)

Settle it. Affirm these words as God's will for your life. Will you pray with me?

Heavenly Father,

I receive the release of your grace, love, and well-being in my life. I fan into a flame the spiritual gift that was imparted to me. God, I know you have not given me a spirit of fear, so I renounce the counsel of fear. Father, I thank you for restoring what this thief has stolen from me.

You have given me the Holy Spirit, who gives power, authority, love, and a sound mind filled with good judgment. This day I choose love. I'm not ashamed of the gospel, I will not shrink back in fear, and I will love fearlessly.

Discussion Questions

1. What are some ways in which you could love more fearlessly?
2. Is there a problem in your marriage that you have labeled as your spouse's problem rather than "our" problem?
3. Are there areas where a lack of vulnerability has translated to a lack of love? What steps can you take to change this?

4. Where are the areas of life where you have equated *making* a mistake with *being* a mistake?

5. Is there a place where you've fallen and been afraid to get back up? Be open about it with a friend or loved one.

6. Outline the difference between a fearless woman and a careless woman.

8

Deep Wells and Wishing Wells

Trials teach us what we are; they dig up the soil,
and let us see what we are made of.

Charles Spurgeon

I am going to assume you want to be a daughter of depth.
If you want depth, you can expect some digging.

I agree with Charles Spurgeon: trials are indeed
a revelation. At least mine are. They are meant to be our
teachers, but at the end of the day, it is up to us to choose
what kind of students we want to be. There are many days
when I get a D—poor but passing. When this happens, I
usually go for a retake. The truth is even though I don't do
life perfectly, I want to do it well. I have the power to choose
whether tests and trials will serve as messengers or simply
leave me looking messy.

We have *little* to *no* control over what happens to us or
what is said about us, but we are far from helpless when it

comes to our actions. We have the power of choice, which gives us total control over our response. And while we are quoting Spurgeon, let's go ahead and dive in a bit deeper to what he suggested our response to trials should look like.

"I've learned to kiss the wave that slammed me into the rock."

This is an unconventional, unexpected response to the things that catch us unaware. Recently, I watched as my granddaughter Sophia played in the waves. She reveled in the wonder of taking each wave head-on. No matter how many times the waves knocked her over and she found herself submerged . . . it was all a game. Laughing, she found her feet, wiped her eyes, and emerged, ready to meet the next one.

Spurgeon is not referring to a rocky coastline but to Christ the rock. Each day is a new opportunity to determine how we will respond to life's waves. If we become defensive, then any issue that comes to light will remain a problem. If we humble ourselves, then the trial allows the Holy Spirit to increase our depth and therefore our capacity for godliness. The challenges of life reveal *what we are made of* without undermining *who we are*. Our identity is established "in Christ," based on what he did rather than what we do or have done. Trials position us to grow more Christlike and therefore unshakable. Christ is the proverbial rock that is higher than I. He is our very core, the rock upon which we find rest each night and awaken to stand on each morning. Jesus alone is our constant and center.

Preparing the Soil

Let's move from the sea to solid ground. I live in the beautiful, sometimes green, and often arid landscape of Colorado, so thinking about my life as soil comes easily. Our soil is hard because it is forged in extreme conditions. Even though the soil in my yard is tough, I want my heart to be tender. When I am *overly* distressed by an offense, whether it is petty or looms large, I cannot escape the realization that my soil has been disturbed. Among the unearthed clots I see destructive grubs trying to maneuver their way back undercover. I see the pattern of their work under the surface. I note that while I was unaware they have nibbled at the roots of my marriage and diminished the growth of the flowers of my friendships. When this happens (and it happens more frequently than I'd like), my conversation with the Father might sound something like this:

"Oh no, this is awful! How did this happen? Heavenly Father, do you see that? Did you hear what I just said or even thought?"

He answers, "Lisa, it was a revelation to you, but not to me. These grubs have been in your soil for a while now. The question that now arises is, do you want to keep them and risk your future harvests?"

On closer inspection I can't help but notice the seeds that have yet to sprout. These are the ones that require time. They are the deep promises of God that are yet unfulfilled in my life and family. I begin to wonder if they will ever grow. My Father patiently explains:

This kind of pestilence multiplies rapidly. The choice is always yours; you can spread the dirt of excuses over them and cover up their activity once again. But they will remain. If you want to be rid of this pestilence, you must renounce them in word and deed and give me permission to remove them.

Seeing them for what they truly are, I renounce and confess the sordid grubs of envy, doubt, and the fear of man.

Well done—and while we are at it, do you see those weeds? Let's pluck them out as well. It will be easier while the soil is loose—and let's go ahead and plant the seed of my Word in their place.

Wait a minute . . . now the struggle is real. Unseen grubs are one thing, but removing every hint of visible greenery while I wait for the promise is quite another. I pause to foolishly contemplate leaving some weeds in play for just a while longer. What about only until the new growth has a chance to appear? Without them I will look like an empty expanse of dirt. I counter:

"But Lord, then my soil will look naked and barren."
"Lisa, do you want to *look* fruitful or *be* fruitful?"

And that is the question of this generation. Is how we look more important than what we are? Settling for merely looking fruitful may very well compromise future seasons of growth. What is sown in secret will one day be revealed openly. I heave a sigh.

"Okay, yank them."
"Done."

And there I am with naked soil and yet unashamed because I know his promises will now grow unhindered deep within me. Trials and tribulations clear the ground and remove what impedes future growth. These encounters serve to refine and prepare us for future potential. There are other words that can be easily substituted for the word *trials*. Feel free to insert *auditions, hardships, assessments, pain and suffering, experiments, examinations,* or simply *tests.*

Our strengths and weaknesses are revealed in the discomfort of these experiences. Collectively and individually, these ordeals work to break up the dry and barren places of our souls in preparation for the new thing and the next season. Without this groundwork, much of the water of God's Word will fail to be absorbed into our lives. Our hearts will be like drought-hardened ground that cannot receive water. If the dry soil is not made ready, the rains will run off and we will experience drought in the midst of abundance.

Trials also serve to teach us who God is.

There was a time I would have argued with you about the purpose of trials. I would have told you that if you were living according to the Word, nothing bad could happen to you. I was young and foolish and indoctrinated with something that would not weather the test of time. I thought the teaching was deep, when really it only prepared me for life in the shallows.

Everything we need for life and godliness is truly found in the Word of God, but it is the trials of life that drive us to our knees so that this truth can be worked in and through our lives. In this posture, the Word of God is no longer read as suggestions for life's best practices but as the very words of life.

Excavate My Life

It was a short and confusing season in my life, mainly because I preferred pretending and burying things. I was young and newly saved and newly married and the turning of my soil had yet to begin. There were just a few scratches on the surface. I remember when it all changed. I was deep into a time of intimate worship and prayer. I foolishly imagined that because I was sitting in the front row of a church as a newly minted pastor's wife that only a few things needed to be addressed in my life. In full confidence, I invited God to *excavate* my life. Twenty-four hours hadn't passed before I was regretting my choice of words.

> *Dear heavenly Father,*
> *Did I say excavate? Can I take it back? That was but a*
> *passionate moment filled with poor word choices. What*
> *I meant to say was landscape and accessorize my life.*

He did not allow the retraction. *Excavation* had been a Spirit-led word choice. Like so many Christians, I lived with deep longings and shallow prayers. Before this dangerous moment in worship, my prayer times had left me feeling empty. The words I whispered were not a catalyst in my life, because I was still praying out of duty rather than devotion. I prayed how I had heard others pray. Yes, I had been told that prayer was simply talking to God, but I couldn't help imagining myself in a throne room surrounded by angelic beings who listened in and found my puny words ridiculous.

Because of this mind-set I didn't know how to frame my prayers with words that could harness the tempest of raw desperation raging within me. Neither did I know what to do with my desperate aching hunger for something more. Since then I have learned that God will use trials to deepen my prayers. Before I gave God permission to (cringe) excavate my life, I didn't know how to allow God to work something deeper within me. Any difficulty or trial was immediately bound! Rather than assail the trial I was binding myself to my old habit patterns and captivity. If they persisted, I ran. If running didn't work, then I hid in the hope of wishing them away.

The hardships of my life had left me frightened and angry. I was hard on others and even harder on myself. Lovely one, if you are doing this, listen, this life is far too difficult for you to be hard on yourself. Over the course of a few decades I have learned that Spurgeon was right. With a vantage point that has been tempered by time I can see that the Word of God tells us *whose* we are and our response to trials definitely reveals *what* we are made of. Trials have the power to transform us from who we are into *who we long to be*. But along the way we picked up the lie that we could be heroes without ever engaging in a battle.

Deep Wells

I love it when someone I am about to meet is referred to as a deep well. It means there is so much more to them than what is on the surface. Deep wells are mysterious and they have stories to tell and I love stories. They are people who have been through stuff that would have muddied or polluted other wells, but their water remained untainted. Deep wells become fountains as they bring refreshing to others. A deep well means they have a greater capacity to reflect. When you talk to a deep well, you may possibly learn more about yourself than you learn about the well.

I know some women who are deep wells. These are always the women I want to know better. When I am around them, I initially feel shy, because I still have so many questions. I prefer to listen rather than to talk when I am in the proximity of a deep well. There is always so much more to hear than what is actually being said. I want to be a deep well, and yet there are times and areas in my life where I still resemble more of a puddle.

Sometimes getting to know a deep well requires heart work on my part. They are not really interested in the books I've written or the conferences I've spoken at. Most of them have been there and done that. They probe further. They don't want to hear how I am pouring out; they want to know how I choose to fill myself. They ask about my husband, my children, my grandchildren, and my heart. They know where to gently poke and probe. Before I realize what I've done, I will violate every one of my personal security boundaries and tell them all. (A practice my husband is not fond of.)

I don't spill my guts under threat of pain; I do it at hints of kindness.

As I've met with these deep wells, I've discovered a few things. Becoming a deep well takes a healthy involvement with life. Depth cannot be purchased—it must be pursued. It comes when we are brave enough to be honest. In that sense, depth is more like a muscle that is developed through consistent use.

Wishing Wells

Recently, John and I were approached by a casting agency. An entertainment conglomerate was in the process of pulling together a television show that would speak from a more spiritual perspective to some of the deeper issues we are facing in our world today. This was not the first time we had been approached for this type of show. After a few offers by other agents who were looking for reality shows, I knew I didn't want to be part of a spectacle. I told my staff that I really didn't think it was a fit. But this casting agent assured my staff this time the show was different. The producers wanted a vehicle that would put their audience in remembrance of the days when people went to their local church when they needed answers. Reluctantly, we agreed to explore the idea a bit further.

John was in one city and I was in another, but we agreed to a conference call. They asked a number of questions that we answered directly and frankly. I for one did not expect to get another call, but we did. They said they liked our energy and were wondering about taking the interview process to the next level. This would entail an hour-long recorded Skype call. They sent us a list of questions they hoped we could address for them in the interview. The first one went something like this:

> My sixteen-year-old daughter is having sex with her older, more sexually experienced boyfriend. He is her first. As a mother, should I have her tested or simply put her on birth control? What should I do?

In my mind, this was a no-brainer. The daughter was an underage girl living in her parents' house. I felt confident with my answer.

I explained the Bible said to flee fornication, not facilitate it. I recommended the family have a sit-down to explain why she and this young man would not be seeing each other anymore . . .

Before I could unpack the concept further, the casting agent interrupted me. She explained that (a) they were going to continue to have sex, and (b) they didn't want us quoting the Bible. They just wanted spiritual advisors. She further explained the agency had come up with questions and this one was from her. It was her sister having sex and her mother who wanted to know what to do. At that point, we realized this interview didn't need to go any further.

The agency knew we were Bible teachers, but they didn't want us to tell them what the Bible said. They wanted us to be deep and spiritual but not biblical. Is there even such a thing? Is there any true wisdom outside of God's counsel? It made me wonder if I had quoted a New Age guru if that would have been admissible. What they wanted from us were shallow answers that sounded deep—a wishing well.

They wanted to avoid conflict. They did not want us to offend anyone by saying something might be wrong. They wanted us to bless the wrong and tell them their evil was good. Their mind-set was "it is what it is" so say what you need to that makes it right. Strike a compromise while at the same time sounding close enough to truth. They also didn't want Christian belief to be overt; they encouraged us to keep it covert. To them that meant God is great, but let's leave Jesus and the Bible out of the mix.

In other words, I'm sure they would have liked me to say something like this: "Yes, be a loving mother and have your daughter tested immediately for STDs. But while you are there put her on some form of long-term birth control to protect her from pregnancy. Then the next time her boyfriend is over, you and your husband can tell him how much you treasure your daughter. Tell him you respect the fact that he is older and more sexually experienced. Ask him if he would be kind enough to accept this package of condoms as a gift from your family to him. That way you will have done all you could to be certain that he does not pass an STD on to her."

Do you see how ludicrous this advice is? But I get it. These producers didn't want to hear biblical truth; they wanted a wishing well. In effect, they were telling John and me, "We will throw you guys some pennies, and in return you will grant the people their wishes. Bless their sin and make them feel good about themselves."

I am afraid far too many Christians have settled for being wished well rather than hearing what they need to develop a deep well. There are far too many women with deep longings but shallow lives. They know the worldly advice they follow is merely an empty echo of their own voices, but they imagine that is all there is . . . so they settle for a well of empty wishes. When they reflect on their lives . . .

They wish they had not said this.

They wish they had not done that.

They wish they had not married him.

They wish they had married him.

They wish they had gone to school.

They wish they had more friends.

They wish they could look like her.

They wish they had not purchased this.

They wish they could purchase that.

They wish they prayed more.

They wish they read their Bible more.

They wish they were more disciplined.

They wish they were more patient.

If only wishing made it so, then we would all be brilliant, beautiful, strong, and brave. Walt Disney told us, "A dream is a wish your heart makes when it is fast asleep." I believe this is true, but the dream and wish only become a reality when you do something with the dream when you are awake. The wish or desire drives the *dream* and we drive the *do*. It is not enough to wish it were well . . . you must *do* well. That is where depth is developed.

The Dangers of Deception

Let no one deceive himself. If anyone among you thinks that he is *wise in this age*, let him become a fool that he may become wise. For the *wisdom of this world is folly* with God. For it is written, "He catches the wise in their craftiness," and again, "The Lord knows the thoughts of the wise, that they are futile." (1 Cor. 3:18–20)

I know it says *let no one deceive himself*, but we all know a woman can deceive herself just as easily. But why would anyone, male or female, want to pull the wool over their own eyes and con themselves? The answer is that no one willingly wants to be deceived. As my husband always says, *the problem with deception is that it is deceiving.*

Deception causes things, people, circumstances, and counsel to appear differently than they truly are. Deception can make submission to God look like legalistic bondage. Deception can make an enemy of your soul sound like a friend. Deception can go as far as to make *evil* look *good* and *good* look *evil*. The power of deception is that it muddies the waters until everything is so blurred you are not sure what to believe. God knew we would find ourselves in this position, so he gave us a standard that would not vary with the passage of time and the shifts of human culture and sentiment. Our standard is the Word of God, and the godly are the standard-bearers.

The choice is ours—do we want the wisdom of this age or ageless wisdom? Whenever the created imagine themselves smarter than their Creator, they are immersed in self-deception. The Word of God alone has the power to give us clarity when circumstances have muddied the water. Without the counsel of Scripture, you will mistakenly call foolishness wisdom.

When this happens, you run the risk of errant beliefs and imagining the underhanded and cunning to be open and honest. Remember the serpent's wisdom is wrapped in the subtle and cunning.

Do we want the wisdom of this age or ageless wisdom?

Subtlety persuades its adherents by alluding to one thing when all the while it really means to accomplish quite another. The serpent masqueraded as an ally with inside information for Adam and Eve. Pretending to be a forthright friend who cared, he implied that both Adam and Eve would become more godlike once they were enlightened to know good from evil. He promised that they could ascend to this level without submitting to the wisdom of God. Adam and Eve did not want to be deceived; they wanted what the serpent promised. They chose to believe that God had lied rather than reject that what the serpent said was not the truth. The serpent promised they would be more godlike when really they became rather godless. Scripture warns us:

> Even if everyone else is a liar, God is true. (Rom. 3:4 NLT)

The way out of deception is repentance; it is when we call our wisdom foolishness and humble ourselves before the eternally wise one. Repentance happens when we turn from the lie to lay hold of the truth.

Satan's subtle promises echo throughout our earth today. Long ago the serpent's suggestions sounded kinder, gentler, and much more inclusive than God's command. After all, which sounds better to you? Eat and die, or eat and gain wisdom? The serpent uses our human pride and folly against us. Who doesn't want to believe that we are wiser than we really are? So he flatters. The truth is that outside of Christ there is no true wisdom. All we can draw on is limited insight from our temporal, earthly perspective.

> Now the Spirit expressly says that in later times some will depart from the faith by devoting themselves to deceitful spirits and teachings of demons. (1 Tim. 4:1)

The deceitful spirit will always tell you that there is enlightenment outside of God's Word. That we are in a new age and God no longer means what he once said. These spirits echo the words of the serpent: don't listen to God; be your own god. Too many miss this by thinking that deception is isolated to overt witchcraft and Satan worship. However, more often than not the deceitful spirits and demons allude to one thing when they are after quite another. If you are a Christian, they can't take your soul, so they will do all they can to strip you of your authority and pollute your well. So much of what is actually godless in this world has become common in our age. We are strongly warned:

> Have nothing to do with irreverent, silly myths. *Rather train yourself for godliness*; for while bodily training is of some value, *godliness is of value* in *every way*, as it holds *promise* for the *present* life and also for the life to *come*. (1 Tim. 4:7–8)

Don't make the mistake of imagining these myths are childish or harmless just because they have been described as irreverent and silly. They are neither. These are not fairy tales or fables woven within a fantasy to teach us a truth; they are doctrines of demons sent to kill, steal, and destroy us.

There is no true wisdom outside the realm of God's counsel.

Jesus never stops with *what we want to hear*; he goes deeper and tells us *what we need to hear*.

Drawing from Our Well

There is a very real well within each of us. It is our soul, the place we draw from. Jeremiah calls it a cistern:

> For my people have done two evil things: They have abandoned me—the fountain of living water. And they have dug for themselves cracked cisterns that can hold no water at all! (Jer. 2:13 NLT)

Our soul-wells can range from very shallow to very deep; the water level may rise or fall according to our capacity. It doesn't matter how deep a well is . . . if the cistern is cracked, it will not hold water. Over time a well can be deepened as well as strengthened and reinforced. Like a well, our soul is a vessel or container. In it we keep our deepest longings, fears, and desires.

Sometimes the water of the well of my soul feels stagnant. Other times I can actually sense its flow, but the water is always there whether the well is empty, half full, or overflowing. In ancient days, enemies would fill wells with dirt because they understood water was the source of life. Rough patches in life can do the same.

When we feel like our well has been overwhelmed, we can open it up by allowing the deepest sorrows or longings of our souls to find their voice. When I feel murky, muddy, and possibly even mean, sometimes all it takes is a song to open my well and refresh my soul. Laughing and spending time with family and godly friends fill the cistern. Reading the Word, keeping a journal, and prayer refresh me like a long drink from a cool fountain on a hot day.

Women with a Past

All of us have a past. Some of our pasts are just more flagrantly colorful than others. Some of us have a good past. Others of us have a horrible past. It is not really a matter of whether the past was cruel or kind to you; the greater danger lies in trying to live in what is gone. We were not created to live in shadows of glory or shame. We were created to live in the light of now as we look to a future of increasing brightness. That is the way of the righteous.

I have learned that human nature tends to look back and have conversations about the past while God is looking forward and declaring our future. It is good to hear people's stories, but to move forward it is more important that we know their dreams.

As I have traveled and spoken, I have had the privilege of declaring hope over thousands of women. I wish you could see the light of understanding illuminate their faces when I declare boldly:

> The attacks on your life have more to do with who you might be in the future than who you have been in the past.

Suddenly, they realize their story isn't over. They realize there is something strategic about their life and that the enemy has targeted them methodically and intentionally. In that moment, they realize what I need you to know. It is *never* about your past. It is *always* about your future. Yes, there are consequences to our choices. I get that. But no matter what you have done God has already gone before you and made a way where there seems to be no way.

You look back and imagine that your actions have closed the only door you will ever have. Guess what. That's a lie. Yes, that door is closed, but if you turn around, you will find another one awaits you. It may look different, it may even be harder, but if you work with God, he will always get you where you need to be. He will always give you the tools you need to create a deep and reinforced well to draw from.

The problem is too many of us sit down near a cracked and shallow wishing well, and cry. We say, "I wish I hadn't done that! I have blown everything!"

Impossible! You, my beautiful friend, are not that powerful. Being a woman with a past does not mean you cannot have a future. Being a woman with a past does not give people the right to control your future. God has control of your future. St. Augustine gives us good counsel on how to start deepening our wells:

> Do you wish to rise? Begin by descending. You plan a tower that will pierce the clouds? Lay first the foundation of humility.

Jesus longs to meet with us at our lowest point and not once but many times. Too often we understand the need to meet him in that initial moment of salvation, only to think he has left us to build on our own from there. Nothing could be further from the truth. We meet him first as the Lord of salvation and then repeatedly, with humility, as the one who restores our souls and patches up the cracked cisterns of our hearts.

Drowning in the Shallows

When I was training to be a lifeguard, I learned that each year a majority of people drown within reach of safety. The three highest-risk groups are the very young (five and under), the young and reckless (males age twenty to twenty-five), and the elderly (over sixty). Interestingly, nearly half of the drowning victims die within six feet of safety. They panic and fail to re-alize how to use their surroundings. This is the very reason a large percentage of people actually drown in three feet or less of water. If they had the presence of mind, they could put their feet down and actually stand up until help came, or they could use the bottom to bob, or they might even walk out of the water to safety. It is not always the depth that kills; it is panicking in the shallows when the unexpected happens. The reckless ones do not respect the water and imagine themselves invincible.

So let's not be a generation of women who drown in the shallows. Let's allow the Holy Spirit to dig deep.

Living Well

When this earthly life is finished, we all hope to hear *well done*. The word *well* describes *how* we do whatever it is we are called to do. There is no such thing as *perfectly done* in the scheme of human life or love. There are only imperfect people doing it well. This word *well* is a gift to each of us. It is a word that means healthy and sound. It describes people who fail and fall, but each time they get back up. We must always get up one more time than we fall.

This is the posture we need to adopt if we want to develop a depth that will sustain us. Listen to how The Passion Translation pens Proverbs 24:16:

> For the lovers of God may suffer adversity
> And stumble seven times,
> But they will continue to rise
> Over and over again.

Adversity is life's university. The cost of each class's tuition can be measured by what it takes for you to get up *just one more time.* Getting up, looking in the mirror, and admitting you messed up can be tough, and even expensive. But to the unrighteous stumbling is fatal.

> But the unrighteous are
> Brought down by just one calamity
> And will never be able to rise again.

I remember watching the lives of two brilliant and gifted leaders who had both stumbled and fallen in similar ways and yet responded very differently to their restoration process.

One pastor submitted to the plan that his board and the restoration team had laid out for him. This plan required a lot from the leader, his wife, and his family. They laid everything down and moved from the city where they were surrounded by friends and had lived for so long, leaving behind the church they had planted. They joined a new church family who would help them navigate their healing. They walked away from everything they knew, believing this approach would be the best way for everyone to heal.

I am sure there were times when they felt they'd been asked to do too much or were treated unfairly. I know they were wounded by the scorn of those whom they had considered friends. When people are involved, there is always margin for error. But they kept their hearts clear of offense and chose to live each day looking forward rather than looking back.

John shared a meal with this leader when he was in his quiet season resting, serving, learning, and healing. Time passed; they kept going forward. This couple is healthy, their marriage is whole, and their children are flourishing. They are closely related to a large church-planting organization in America. This connection affords them an avenue to openly share their life lessons, to help other leaders heal, and to prevent other leaders from stumbling in the same way they did. I loved them before, but my respect for them has grown. I am so thankful they didn't stay down. They got up over and over again. It was hard, but they stayed the course.

The other leader and his wife took a very different approach. I remember early on John had a text conversation with this leader. In it John encouraged him that no matter what happened to stay the course. He agreed. But adversity happened and they didn't. They decided to opt out of the process. They felt what their leaders asked was unreasonable and that they had been treated unfairly. Which may have been true on some levels . . . only Jesus knows.

The tragedy is that their offense pulled them back down into the mire of what they had already been through. They became experts on how they were mishandled. Sadly, we lost the benefit of what they had learned through their journey.

The second way a fall takes you out is when you choose to see your stumble as a life sentence rather than a life lesson. The fact that you've failed doesn't make you a failure. If you are alive, *you will* encounter adverse circumstances. Don't assume some people are exempt. Some people just carry the wear and tear of hardship more graciously than others do. I have seen enough to know there is no avoiding it. People will hurt or disappoint you; some do it on purpose, and others will do so unknowingly. Life will wound or at best inconvenience you. Adversity happens to everyone at some time and on some level. Here is a beautiful truth. There were many things that at the time were so painful I thought I would never forget them. And yet most of these are now things I can barely remember. Why? I got up and continued to walk. As I have walked, new adversities have waylaid me. So much water has passed under my bridge that the very things I thought I'd never be able to rise above in my thirties provided me with a master's degree in life in my fifties.

Each of our stumbles is another chance to learn. We begin to recognize obstacles and hazards. We make sure our shoelaces are tied. We read the Word so the path before us is lit. Each time we rise, our capacity increases. Our wells get deeper, making more room for the living waters of the Holy Spirit.

A Faithful Finish

Now let's look at the second meaning of our word *well*. A well speaks of a water source such as a spring or fountain. When we draw our life and strength from the fount of living water we become a source of refreshing for others. Deep wells of living water know that their source is inexhaustible. Then when people look at us, they don't see a scattering of copper pennies in the shallow water. They see the unfathomable faithfulness of God.

The *done* part of *well done* is all about the *completion*. The Bible is rife with stories and parables about finishing well—or poorly. There is Noah, a man whose great boat-building project took years. There is Samson, who despite a colossal blunder finished in a spectacular show of divine strength. There is Peter, whose denial of Christ, and Paul, whose persecution of Christ, paved the way for the power of their ministries. In contrast, there is the man who started his building without first counting the costs. He began well but then was mocked for not finishing (Luke 14:27–29). Then there was the servant who was entrusted with one talent, which he decided to bury until his master's return. Coins don't grow in the ground, so when he dug it up all he had was what he started with. Ending where he began earned him the label of wicked and a place on the outside looking in (Matt. 25:14–30).

> It is ultimately not about our pace but about how we finish our race.

What all these stories tell us is that it is ultimately not about our *pace* but about how we finish our *race*. Persistent, faithful, steady obedience will always win out over casual and inconsistent bursts of activity and enthusiasm, and if we stumble along the way, and even if we fall, if we pick ourselves up and head in the right direction, God will bring us home.

Journeying well in this life requires us to dig deep, reinforced wells, which requires a commitment to *finish* what we start, faithfully. Anyone can create a wishing well, but we want to dig *deep* wells, cisterns of life that are reinforced with God's Word and renewed with the refreshing fountains of the Spirit. That's where God's great reward—a life and a promise without rival—can be found.

Discussion Questions

1. What is an area that God is currently "excavating" in your life?

2. How would you describe a woman who is a deep well?

3. Is it possible to be spiritual without being biblical?

4. What fills the well of your soul? What empties it?

5. How can you be more intentional about tending your well?

9

A Daughter without Rival

The tyrant dies and his rule is over, the martyr dies and his rule begins.

Søren Kierkegaard

This woman:

Defied the most powerful and perverse ruler in the world.

Gave a bold presentation of the gospel that was considered incomparable.

Was beaten, tempted, and tortured in every way imaginable and yet remained steadfast to the gospel, her friends, and her Lord.

Was imprisoned but her reach could not be contained.

Was single but far from alone.

Was numbered among the apostles, and early church historians say her ministry was nearly unrivaled in signs and wonders.

You may be wondering why you don't know her.

I understand. I only recently met her myself. She is but one of the many women who were church mothers whose names were buried by the sands of time. Over the course of my life I had heard whispers of her exploits. I wanted to meet her. I wasn't content for her to remain a rumor, so I searched resources on church history to find her. In my pursuit, I called Bible scholars, researched online, and purchased books. Once I discovered her name, I was able to assemble enough pieces to make her acquaintance. Once I knew more about her, I thought it only right that you should meet her as well.

Her name is Photina, or at times Photini. Her name is Greek and means "the enlightened one." It was the name she adopted when she was baptized into the Christian faith. As he did with all of us, Jesus flooded her world with a revelation of light. As a devout believer in Christ, she was numbered with those who were gathered in the upper room. When the Holy Spirit came upon their number in power, she was there; a tongue of fire rested on her, and she was filled with the Spirit and began to speak in another language. On Pentecost Photina received the commission to preach the gospel to the ends of the earth.

Our brave sister left behind everything that represented the limits and the comfort of the life she had known and traveled to the distant land of Africa. She didn't go alone—she brought most of her family along. Her encounter with Christ wrought such a compelling transformation in her life that both of her sons and all five of her sisters were also converted. Photina, her son Joseph, and her sisters journeyed to the uttermost parts of their world, just as Jesus commanded in Acts 1:8.

In Africa, they all labored faithfully, spreading the gospel of Christ in Carthage, producing astounding fruit. When news reached them that Nero, deranged emperor, was arresting and persecuting Christians throughout his realm, Photina sought God's wisdom. Jesus appeared to her in a dream and instructed her to go to Rome and confront him. So rather than move beyond Nero's reach, they headed straight into the eye of the storm. Immediately, Photina, her son, and her sisters set sail for Rome in the company of a large contingent of Carthaginian Christians.

They were warned there would be consequences if they chose to openly live their Christian faith and were admonished to practice a private form of worship. Here is a conversation between her son Victor, who served as a Roman officer, and an official named Sebastian.

> "Victor, I know that you, your mother, and your brother are followers of Christ. As a friend I advise you to submit to the will of the emperor. If you inform on any Christians, you will receive their wealth. I shall write to your mother and brother, asking them not to preach Christ in public. Let them practice their faith in secret." Victor replied, "I want to be a preacher of Christianity like my mother and brother." Sebastian said, "O Victor, we all know what woes await you, your mother, and brother."[1]

How many would still practice their faith openly if they knew this decision would mean guaranteed woe? Later her son Victor threw his lot in with his mother, brother, and aunts. Here is an excerpt from the same document cited earlier that lends a window into her first audience with Nero.

> Photini's [Photina's] arrival and activity aroused curiosity in the capital city. "Who is this woman?" they asked. "She came here with a crowd of followers and she preaches Christ with great boldness." Soldiers were ordered to bring her to the emperor, but Photini anticipated them. Before they could arrest her, Photini, with her son Joseph and her Christian friends went to Nero. When the emperor saw them, he asked why they had come. Photini answered, "We have come to teach you to believe in Christ." The half-mad ruler of the Roman Empire did not frighten her. She wanted to convert him![2]

Not surprisingly, Nero was less than receptive. He ordered that those who claimed to be in the hands of Jesus should have their hands beaten with iron rods. The guards took Photina and all those in her company away to be beaten for their impudence. Over the next three hours their hands were brutally beaten with iron rods, but the Christians felt no pain and sang psalms while their torturers exhausted themselves. Not one of the Christ followers had as much as a mark on their hands.

When Nero discovered that the beatings had no effect on them, he imprisoned them and devised a plan to convince Photina and her sisters to convert. This time he intended to turn them to his will with kindness. He ordered six thrones set up in a large banqueting hall. Before these thrones he arranged to have every manner of Roman wealth arrayed before the sisters. No expense was spared in the preparation of a collection that would appeal to the feminine soul. In addition to gold and silver there were jewels and magnificent garments laid out before each woman. These riches and a life of ease and beauty could be theirs if they would only renounce their Christian faith and sacrifice to the Roman deity. To persuade them toward this end, he commissioned his very own daughter, Domnina, to act as his agent.

When Domnina entered the room, she greeted Photina warmly and in the course of her salutation mentioned Christ. Photina mistook her for a fellow believer, and after embracing her, she openly shared the transforming love and wonder of her Christ with the one she presumed to be a sister. Domnina was undone, and rather than refute Photina, she converted to Christianity. But she was not alone in her conversion—her serving girls were converted as well, as they listened to the bold preaching of the gospel by the sisters. Then Photina instructed Domnina and her servants to remove all the wealth from the room and distribute it freely among the poor they found in the streets of Rome. Domnina was baptized and received a new name.

Nero was enraged. He ordered Photina, her sisters, and her sons to be put to death by fire. He had a large furnace constructed, but when they were thrown into the furnace, they wouldn't catch on fire. Next, Nero ordered them executed by poisoning. When the poisoner came, Photina volunteered to be the first in her company to drink, but the toxins had no effect on her or on any of the Christians. Then the one Nero had sent to poison them converted to Christ. They remained imprisoned for their faith, and over the next three years they were beaten and subjected to every form of torture the twisted emperor could invent.

But the more he oppressed them, the more their fame grew. Word of their faith and power spread throughout the empire's capital, and during their prison tenure, the jail itself became a house of worship. Roman citizens came regularly to the cells of the believers to receive prayer and hear the gospel. For three years the message of Christ continued to infiltrate Rome from the confines of the prison, and many believed.

Nero sent for one of his former servants whom he had imprisoned, and the man reported all that was happening. Nero ordered the immediate beheading of all the Christians he held in prison. The only exception was Photina. He hoped to break her resolve through grief and isolation, so he had her removed from the prison and lowered into a deep, dark, dry well. A few of the accounts say she was severely scourged first. He left her there for weeks in what must have felt like an open earthen grave. She was acutely alone. These were dark days for Photina and she wept, but not over the loss of her loved ones. She knew they had been released from every form of earthly prison and already granted a heavenly reception. She grieved that she had been denied the privilege of being martyred alongside her sons and sisters and therefore robbed of a martyr's crown. From all I read it would appear that this time period was the most difficult for her.

Every historical account I read mentioned this season in a well. In one account, she died there in the depths of the dry well, but not from despair but by choice. Like Stephen, she beheld her Savior in a dream and yielded her spirit. Other written records said she was removed from the well after an extended length of time, and after a dream in which Jesus appeared to her, she was released from life while in prison.

Either way this woman's life was a deep well of living water that nourished and refreshed countless others.

Modern-Day Martyrs

Photina did not produce admirers or fans; her life produced witnesses and martyrs. This woman had something I want. She had something we all may need in the days that are before us: unshakable resolve. Church attendance grows when the world looks favorably toward Christians. But committed disciples are birthed in seasons of hardship. Renowned Catholic historian Christopher Henry Dawson explains:

> The Church grew under the shadow of the executioner's rods and axes, and every Christian lived in the peril of physical torture and death. The thought of martyrdom coloured the whole outlook of early Christianity. But it was not only a fear, it was also an ideal and a hope. For the martyr was the complete Christian, he was the champion and hero of the new society and its conflict with the old, and even the Christians who failed in the moment of the trial—the lapsi—looked on the martyrs as their saviours and protectors.[3]

We live in an age rife with perverse wickedness and violence. Every time I think it can get no worse . . . it does. Christians are still being martyred today—and rather than outrage, our world's response betrays a posture of indifference. I am heartbroken, but not in any way surprised. Recently, on American soil, Christian students were martyred for their faith as the gunman systematically shot those who professed Christ in the head and those who did not in the leg. Rather than call it a hate crime, our news media made it an issue of gun control.

If the Bible has been interpreted correctly, then relief and deliverance will not come from any of the leaders of this world. But it does not mean that we remain silent in the face of darkness any more than Photina did. We must be a living, breathing revelation of 1 John 4:4:

> Little children, you are from God and have overcome them, for he who is in you is greater than he who is in the world.

Christians in other nations are beheaded, and the videos of these atrocities are sent out with a global warning to all those who would dare call themselves the *people of the cross*. With this designation I have to wonder if the perpetrators remember who we are and we have forgotten.

Not long ago militant Muslims broke into a gathering of Christians at one of Kenya's colleges and murdered all those who had gathered for a morning prayer meeting. Then the militants pulled students from the area dorms and hostels and at gunpoint questioned their faith. Again, those who had the courage to identify themselves as Christians were shot. Almost 150 people were killed, with many more wounded. The organization that led the assault bragged on its social media channels that this was but the beginning and went on to assure *the people of the cross* that there would be more to come.[4]

It is time we prepare ourselves to suffer for Christ. Better to have our hearts ready to give an answer and be prepared to suffer than to be caught unaware and deny him. We need to have the same outlook as the disciples in Acts 5:41–42:

Then they left the presence of the council, *rejoicing that they were counted worthy to suffer dishonor for the name*. And every day, in the temple and from house to house, they did not cease teaching and preaching that the Christ is Jesus.

Have you ever met someone who was beaten for their faith in Christ? Have you ever spoken with someone who rejoiced that they were worthy to suffer dishonor for *the name*? I have. These saints have a radiant purity in and about their lives, not because they were beaten but because they met Jesus in the fellowship of his sufferings. They are crowned with a grace that I have yet to know. The ones I met labor in fields where being a Christian endangers their lives. They live in peril almost daily. Often these are my precious brothers and sisters who labor to translate our books. The truth is what I write in safety they translate in danger. More often than not I do not even feel worthy to work alongside them. Their very lives put me in remembrance of Paul's words in 1 Corinthians:

> Why are we in danger every hour? I protest, brothers, by my pride in you, which I have in Christ Jesus our Lord, I die every day! (15:30–31)

Western Weakness

Can I be honest? I tremble for the Western church. Sadly, in our day we are more likely to meet those who have dishonored his name. At times, my own apathy and selfishness sickens me.

Recently, John and I had a conversation over dinner with pastors who shared how they are constantly warning their congregations—people who profess to have embraced Jesus

Christ as Lord—against the trappings of sexual immorality. In return, they receive blank looks and weak excuses. Couples who are living together will explain, "We are planning on marrying one day; why is it wrong to live together and have sex now?"

Another minister shared his anguish that a prominent Christian leader was planning to divorce his wife although there were no scriptural grounds for his action. He explained that the man understood that the divorce would take him out of the speaking circuit for possibly a year, but then he'd be right back in with everyone. Sadly, he might be correct. The fear of man does not keep any of us from sin anymore. Only the fear of the Lord will cause us to depart from evil.

After a particularly moving moment in a service in which the Holy Spirit commissioned hundreds of women to take up their cross and follow Jesus, the leader got up and told all the women not to feel any pressure—God didn't need them to *do*; he just needed them to *be*. Really?

I am so thankful that Jesus didn't stop with the title of *being* the Son of God and that he was willing to strip himself of his divine nature and privileges in order to *do* the work of a servant on our behalf. I look at the church and I see it so deeply immersed and entangled with the world that it scares me.

The Woman with a Past

But this is not how it began for Photina. There was a time when she too was so deeply immersed in a sinful lifestyle that she was seen as nothing more than a shamed outsider.

She was a woman with a past living under the jurisdiction of the law that left her without the hope of a future.

Scripture lends us a window into this woman's background. When we first meet her, she is unnamed, divorced, and displaced. Her life was so conflicted on so many fronts that no one imagined she could ever minister. Understanding this, she first shared the gospel as questions and suggestions. Maybe like our friend you too have felt the judgment of others to such an extreme that your statements have remained hints and questions.

Forgive them.

People who would tie you to your past . . . have yet to experience a revelation of God's mercy and the power of the rebirth.

Maybe it is you who question yourself. My past raised a lot of questions for me. And yet it was the darkest, dirtiest places of my life that were later redeemed to become my deepest wells. While it is true that novices should not be promoted to leadership too quickly, every Christian should be encouraged to be a witness of saving power. But Jesus's precious grace should never be abused or used as an excuse to go and sin some more (Rom. 6:1–2). Instead, his grace should propel us to change, to live transformed lives of increasing righteousness and to receive new names.

Before she took on the name "enlightened one," Photina was known to us only by an ethnic designation. We met her when we listened in on her private interchange with Jesus. She is our friend the Samaritan woman. How amazing that the woman who formerly had *five* husbands would one day labor alongside her *five* sisters! I love this, because in the Bible, the number five symbolizes grace. And in her case, she experienced grace upon grace!

I've always loved this woman. For years I've seen her as a woman of great capacity. She was a deep well living a shallow life. The hardships she experienced and the realities of her choices had dug a deep, dark, *dry* hollow within her. The enemy of her soul meant for this to be a perpetually broken place that isolated her and buried her dreams.

When I read the interaction of Jesus and this woman in John 4, I always place myself in the scene. I imagine that the disciples thought it was safe to leave the weary Jesus alone by the well. It was not yet time for the shepherds to bring their flocks in to be watered, and the women of the area had already come for their households' water earlier in the day. I love how The Passion Translation sets up their initial interaction:

> Wearied by his long journey, he sat on the edge of Jacob's well. He sent his disciples into the village to buy food, for it was already afternoon. Soon a Samaritan woman came to draw water. Jesus said to her, "Give me a drink of water." (John 4:6–8)

Jesus is tired from an extensive walk and exhausted by the Pharisees. I see him seated on the edge of Jacob's ancient well. The relentless Middle Eastern afternoon sun beats down on him, but he can feel the cool air rising from the deep well. Jesus looks into its depth and ponders its history as he reviews the events of the day. Their outreach in Judea had ended abruptly and the walk had been long and dusty. He had put an end to the baptisms when he learned that the religious leaders had turned them into some sort of temple numbers competition between his and John's disciples (John 1).

Why couldn't they see it for what it was? They were working together as colaborers. Yes, the masses came. Their hunger was so desperate after so many years of dryness. Now the prophetic and the promise were making a people ready. Lives were being restored through repentance and the flowing waters of baptism.

It was so holy, so hopeful, and they had tried to reduce it to a circus. So he had left behind the waters of the Jordan for this arid plain.

He closes his eyes a moment against the dust and glaring sun. He will rest and wait at this ancient well for the return of his disciples. He releases a heavy sigh. Suddenly, a sense of expectation stirs in his heart and he senses the Holy Spirit whisper, *I have a purpose here in this barren Samaritan field.* Jesus hears one word, *harvest.* He opens his eyes and watches as a lone daughter of Samaria comes to collect water.

She carries a large vessel. It is similar to the ones the other women use when they collect water at the dawn of a day. Her vessel is empty and so is her heart. This daughter had sunk so low that she even avoids the company of women. Bible scholars suggest that she chose to come in the heat of the day when the number of people at the well would be at an all-time low.

He watches her. He notices when she sees him and quickly averts her eyes. By virtue of his clothing she knows he is Jewish. Jews don't associate with Samaritans; they despise them. This woman has known trouble before and she doesn't want trouble again.

Forewarned, she approaches the opposite side of the well, where she lowers her vessel and prepares to draw forth the water. He calls to her. Startled, she lifts her head and stops midmotion. There is something in the tenor and tone of his voice that arrests her. His request for water sounds more like an invitation than a demand. Unsure, she counters:

> Why would a Jewish man ask a Samaritan woman for a drink of water? Jews won't even drink from a cup that a Samaritan has used! (John 4:9 TPT).

Imagine, if you will, a prejudice so profound that using the same glass of water would cause you to be unclean. Not only is she a Samaritan, but she is also a woman. But Jesus is not afraid of sharing her cup . . . he is prepared to drink her cup of wrath for her. Nor does Jesus want to use her like the other men she has known. He wants to make himself known. Maybe he wants the solace of conversation. Maybe he is weary of being misrepresented by the arrogant religious leaders. Perhaps like many of us he finds it comforting to unburden his heart to a stranger.

> Jesus replied, "If you only *knew who I am and the gift* that God is *wanting* to *give* you—you'd be asking me for a drink, and I would give you *living water.*" (v. 10 TPT)

The woman is astonished. Who is this man who speaks of a gifting God? She walks around the well to his side to see what he has in his possession that would empower him to make such an outrageous claim. Maybe his vessel is at his feet? She discovers nothing in his possession that would substantiate his claim. Will this man's promise prove empty like the words of all the other men she has known? Intrigued, she questions his capacity to draw forth this living water.

> But sir, you don't even have a bucket and this well is *very deep.* So where do you find this *"living water"*? (v. 11 TPT)

She reasons that water this refreshing must come from a place deep within the well. Could it be possible that this Jew is insulting Jacob's well? This well is rich in legacy and deeper than most. She pushes her point a bit further.

> Do you really think that you are greater than our ancestor Jacob who dug this well and drank from it himself, along with his children and livestock? (v. 12 TPT)

It is interesting that the well in contention here is Jacob's. The very name *Jacob* means "the one who displaces, deceives, or grasps the heel of." When God prophesied the enmity between the seed of the woman and the seed of the serpent, he said the serpent would strike at her seed's heel. Later in life God changed Jacob's name to *Israel*, which means "prince of God." How thought-provoking that this woman who had been deceived so many times into believing that men could fulfill her thirst finds herself talking to Israel's Prince of Peace at Jacob's well. Even though she is mistaken, Jesus knows exactly what is going on.

This conversation is ultimately about the desperation of her thirst, not the condition of the well. Jesus does what he does best . . . he ignores her questions and speaks directly to her deepest longing.

> *Everyone* who drinks of this water will be thirsty again, but whoever drinks of the water that I will give him will never be thirsty again. *The water that I will give him* will become in him *a spring of water welling* up to eternal life. (John 4:13–14)

Within the word *everyone* Jesus unites all who thirst for more than this earth can provide. He weaves together both

Jew and Samaritan and all those who had ever visited this fount, past and present. Every earthly well ultimately serves to highlight our desperate human thirst. The Passion Translation of John 4:13 reads:

> If you drink from Jacob's well *you'll be thirsty again and again.*

Old wells will leave you thirsty time and time again. Ultimately, only God can quench our thirst. These ancient wells were subject to failure because their source was intimately attached to earthbound conditions. At any given moment an enemy could slip in and lace a well with poison or fill it in with dirt, or a long-lasting drought could dry it up.

Every earthly well ultimately serves to highlight our desperate human thirst.

Like an old well, the law could be easily poisoned by human statutes or buried in the earth of man-made rituals and rules. The Samaritans adhered to only the first five books of the Torah and worshiped at their own mountain. They lived in but a shadow of the law, and yet the Jews proved that even the law in its entirety cannot give us the life we long for. These ancient wells of laws and patriarchs were given to us for the purpose of punctuating our desperate need for the living water of the Holy Spirit. The law requires a location and place of worship. The law places God just *beyond* our reach. The worship of God remains an observance rather than a life source. Under the law there is visitation rather than habitation. The law is where he can be seen from a distance but not touched. The law maintains a Mount Sinai dynamic where we can behold God but not be held by him.

When our sanctuary of worship is *around us* rather than *within us*, we run the risk of remaining outsiders. This encounter between the Samaritan woman and Jesus broke so many legal parameters. This woman had broken the law and was living with a man. Even in our more liberal church day, she would be considered to be "living in sin." And yet Jesus saw beyond her shameful outside and spoke straight into her broken heart.

The law always requires more of you than it can give. Living water cannot be contained or even weighed, for it is liquid light. The same is not true of dead water. If you want more than a drink at Jacob's well, you will need a container. What you take home with you will be limited to what you can carry. Dead water is not light; it is heavy. If we use the recommended daily requirement of sixty-four ounces of water, you can count on four pounds of weight per person. If you are drawing water for cooking, cleaning, bathing, as well as the consumption of a family of four, your load could easily exceed twenty pounds. This measure does not even factor in the weight of your vessel and the distance you would need to walk.

And you would have to make this journey again and again and again. Jesus speaks of a thirst that is perpetual and insatiable. As a daughter of the Middle East growing up in a dry and arid land, this woman has known thirst all her life. There is no well deep enough or water cool enough to satiate her desperate need for love, affirmation, and companionship. Her soul is desperately dehydrated. Time and time again she had been deceived by what she hoped would quench her cravings and refresh her soul. Her longings are valid, but like so many of us, she kept looking for the right thing in all the wrong places.

> It is not wrong to want to be loved.
> It is not wrong to want to build your life with an intimate other.
> It is not wrong to want a life of dignity.
> It is not wrong to want a life of purpose.
> It is not wrong to want friends.
> It is not wrong to want a life of worship.

Jesus does not marginalize her longing, nor will he scoff at yours. He validates her thirst when he promises to satisfy it. He offers her life without end rather than a life of dead ends. Out of the very depth and desperation of her soul she moves closer and pleads:

> Sir, give me this water, so that I will not be thirsty or have to come here to draw water. (John 4:15)

In her anguished plea, I hear hope. I recognize her longing as my own. Jesus, please don't make me come back to this place that continually reminds me of my failures. Like her, I had failed to keep the laws of my youth. She knew she couldn't earn it, didn't deserve it; this could only come to her if it was a gift. Like an addict, she had nothing more to spend. Her thirst had enslaved her.

Before Jesus could give her this living water, he needed to see if she was ready to empty herself. Was she truly ready to leave it behind? He addresses the faulty, stagnant well she had drawn from for so long . . . men.

Jesus said to her, "Go, call your husband, and come here." (v. 16)

Don't imagine that with this directive Jesus was looking for an authority structure through which he could speak to her, nor was he necessarily pointing out her sin. Rather, he asked for her husband to locate her pain. Our brave sister spoke the truth even knowing full well that the truth might very well disqualify her from the rabbi's living water.

I have no husband. (v. 17)

This admission must have weighed heavy on her. Five failed marriages. There is no hint of blame, no suggestion of excuses in her admittance; it is just the raw and ugly truth. I have no husband . . .

Jesus said to her, "You are right in saying, 'I have no husband'; for you have had five husbands, and the one you now have is not your husband. What you have said is true." (vv. 17–18)

Jesus can work with truth tellers and brave confessions. She told her present reality, and he filled in the details of her past. Five men had taken her to wife only to cast her aside. Sometimes I wonder why there has been so much focus on her as the sinner. I am the granddaughter of a woman who was married four times to three husbands. She was not a victim; it was her choice and vice. But it may have not been so with this woman. We don't know for certain that she was in the wrong. She lived under the law, which meant a man could decide that marrying his wife had been a mistake, and he could easily put her away with a certificate that affirmed his disappointment. Under the law it would have been impossible for her to be the one changing husbands of her own initiative. A remarriage would have required this certificate of divorce. Can you imagine . . . five times a failure? Now this woman is so broken that she is willing to live with a man with whom she shares a bed but not a name. Her life is consumed by appetites that refused to be satisfied. Her spirit is broken and yet she hopes. John 4:19 continues:

> The woman said to him, "Sir, I perceive that you are a prophet."

Until recently, I didn't understand the weight of this admission. She was stepping out beyond all she had known because Samaritans believed that only Moses was a prophet. According to Matthew 10:41, this reception positioned her to receive a prophet's reward: "The one who receives a prophet because he is a prophet will receive a prophet's reward."

What is this prophet's reward? I believe this gift can be expressed in many ways, but there is none more precious than a revelation and realization of living truth. Prophets are also referred to as seers. Everywhere Jesus went he opened up the eyes of understanding. When she chose to receive Jesus as a prophet, she looked to her future and asked Jesus where she should worship. I can only imagine that she was weary of her old life with its old ways. She had no way of knowing that a new hour was upon her that would redefine worship as a person rather than a place.

> Jesus said to her, "Woman, believe me, the hour is coming when neither on this mountain nor in Jerusalem will you worship the Father." (v. 21)

In The Passion Translation, the Aramaic opens this verse up a bit further for us with:

Believe me, dear woman, the time has come when you won't worship the Father on a mountain nor in Jerusalem, but in your heart.

She honors Jesus as the prophet he truly is, and in return Jesus calls forth what she truly is, *dear*. This term means "beloved and cherished, prized, precious and priceless, valued and treasured." I have to wonder the last time she had been called by any term of endearment. He was rebuilding her broken heart and wounded spirit with words of destiny.

Even now I hear Jesus inviting each and every one of his daughters, "Believe me, my valued, treasured, and loved woman, your time has come . . ." Your time to believe is now. Pause a moment. What has he whispered to your soul?

Our God is not closest to you on a mountain, in a city, or even at a church. No individual can keep you from his presence. Thankfully, no mistake can separate you from what abides within you. Jesus awaits your worship at the well of your heart. The Scriptures remind us that our God is as close as a whisper:

But what does it say? "The word is near you, in your mouth and in your heart." (Rom. 10:8)

Jesus shared this revolutionary concept with a woman at her lowest. Who had ever heard of a God without the limits of location? A God who was willing to meet with her wherever she was? Imagine how wonderful this news would have been to her. She is an outcast from her people and an outsider to the Jews, but God had made a place for himself within the sanctuary of her heart. Just as she has been forthright and revealed who she is, the Son of God is about to be just as open and revealing with her. Her choices had pushed her to the outer limits of life. Jesus invites her in. Jesus goes on to explain:

> You worship what you do not know; we worship what we know, for salvation is from the Jews. *But the hour is coming, and is now here, when the true worshipers will worship the Father in spirit and truth, for the Father is seeking such people to worship him.* God is spirit, and those who worship him must worship in spirit and truth. (John 4:22–24)

Jesus shatters her traditions with truth. If what this rabbi is saying is true, then *she* is just the type of worshiper his Father is looking for: those who long to worship both in spirit and in truth.

We miss the irony of it because we know and accept all of what Jesus was unpacking as understood truth, but at the time these concepts were radical. More than likely she had never heard of God the Father. The Passion Translation of John 4:22–23 reads:

> From here on to worship the Father is not a matter of the *right place* but with *the right heart*. For God is a Spirit, and He *longs to have sincere worshippers who worship and adore him in the realm of the Spirit and in truth.*

She could connect with a God who longed. I believe at this very moment she was conflicted with glorious hope in the face of what she had known as an oppressive religion. She is not sure what to believe; her heart is trembling with hope, confusion, and wonder, but the one thing she knows she shares.

The woman said to him, "I know that Messiah is coming (he who is called Christ). When he comes, he will tell us all things." (v. 25)

I wonder if Jesus found her childlike faith irresistible. He couldn't hold the good news of the truth back from her any longer. I picture him holding her gaze as he whispers:

I who speak to you am he. (v. 26)

He did exactly what she expected the Messiah to do . . . he told her all things. Sometimes even without saying everything, our God addresses all things. Be still my heart. Our Christ, the anointed one, often answers our questions about worship by telling us the truth about ourselves. In one fell swoop, he exposes foolish traditions and cuts away human reasoning with his sword of truth. Who wouldn't drop their water jar and run after hearing this? That is our Jesus. He doesn't shame the shamed. He takes them into his confidence and shares with them the noble things the Pharisees (and even his disciples at times) refused to hear.

The moment is over. The disciples return and are troubled by the discovery that Jesus has been talking to a woman who is only worthy of their disdain. But their reception no longer matters to her. Once you have been received by God . . . what is the rejection of man to you? It is interesting to note that not one of the disciples had invited the Samaritans out to see Jesus. That was okay because Jesus had already sent his messenger. She was the one he had in mind all along.

So the woman left her water jar and went away into town and said to the people, "Come, see a man who told me all that I ever did. Can this be the Christ?" They went out of the town and were coming to him. (vv. 28–30)

On close examination we will find she is intentional with her words. She doesn't call him a prophet or mention that he is a Jew, knowing that both of these might cause the townspeople to reject him. She uses her own testimony to open the way for them. I love that our friend invites them to *come and see* rather than suggest that they come and hear. Seeing can mean believing, and when your eyes are opened, you want everyone else to see as well.

I love that Jesus chose to reveal something so preemptive, precious, and holy to a woman others saw as tainted, common, and soiled. By speaking the mysteries of God to someone others considered the lowest of the low, he threw the door open for us all. For this very reason I have visited her story in more than one of my books. I always see their interaction from a different angle, but never with an indifferent heart.

For years I have loved this intimate encounter that made the shamed outsider an ultimate insider. For a time I even liked the fact that she was nameless; that way I could easily insert my name into her story. That was until I learned to know her by Photina, the enlightened. She started evangelizing that very day in Samaria, but as you now know, her reach extended far beyond that region's borders.

Her story should encourage each of us who are deep wells living shallow lives. What else could possibly explain a wayward woman conversing with a prophet about worship? Her well was not only deep . . . it was also dry. She'd had five husbands and two sons and yet the longing remained. This woman with huge capacity had poured herself out completely until the very marrow of her bones ached.

Suddenly, it was different. She knew the gift. Jesus had invited her, and she boldly asked for living water. This magnificent Messiah knew her completely and loved her unreservedly. So at his invitation this daughter without rival drank deeply of his living water and went on to become Photina, evangelist and apostle, who walked into danger with unshakable resolve.

Woman with a past, will you follow her lead?

Discussion Questions

1. Are you hungry for more of the power of God in your life?
2. How were you impacted by the story of Photina?
3. Don't you love that she was the woman at the well? What promise does this hold for us?
4. Are there areas in your life where you are a deep well living a shallow life?

10

A Life Unrivaled

You are never too old to set another goal or dream
a new dream.

C. S. Lewis

I want to share yet another ancient story of courage and
devotion with you. There once was a beautiful young
virgin named Thecla.[1] She chanced to overhear the gospel as Paul preached in a neighboring house. She sat perched
by her window transfixed as she listened to Paul's call to the
young men and women to worship Christ in chastity and
virtue. Thecla was betrothed, but when she heard Paul's
words, she decided to spurn the arranged marriage and live
out the remainder of her days for the glory of God. Paul
was oblivious to his influence on Thecla, but her decision
did not go over well with her mother and her fiancé, who
used their influence to stir up an angry mob against Paul.

The civil unrest landed Paul before one of the governors of Iconium, who had him immediately imprisoned.

Grief stricken, Thecla used pieces of jewelry to bribe her way into the prison to meet Paul and hear the gospel of Jesus directly. When her family discovered their missing daughter in Paul's prison cell, they had both of them brought before the governor. Paul was scourged then cast outside the city. Thecla's mother denounced her, and the young woman was condemned to death. She would be burnt at the stake to serve as an example to any other daughters who might consider such wanton rebellion.

As Thecla went to her death, Paul gathered with other Christians outside the city in the catacombs and prayed earnestly. Thecla was bound to the stake, but when the flame was lit, she didn't catch on fire. Then a storm of unusual violence arose, the downpour put out the flames at her feet, and Thecla was delivered from death. Afraid that it was a sign from the Greek gods, the authorities released her and put her out of the city. Disowned, Thecla met up with the other banished Christians who had decided to travel in the company of Paul to Antioch.

No sooner had they entered the city when a man of great influence and power named Alexander was drawn to Thecla's beauty and tried to purchase her from Paul. When Paul refused, he tried to take her by force. Thecla fought back violently and in the process removed Alexander's crown of laurel leaves and spurned him publicly, as she commanded him not to touch a handmaiden of God.

Outraged, Alexander dragged her before the governor of Antioch. In the dispute, Thecla admitted tearing Alexander's clothes as she tried to escape. Again, she was condemned to die. Her execution was set for the following day, and this time she was to be torn and eaten by wild beasts.

The women of Antioch were outraged. They felt the judgment against Thecla was unjust. A Roman woman of noble birth stepped forward and requested that Thecla be allowed to stay in her home rather than in the prison to protect her virginity. Over the course of the evening the older and younger women became close friends.

The next morning the noblewoman wept bitterly as Thecla was chained behind a fierce lioness and led off to an arena. The crowd roared as Thecla was stripped and forced into a stadium filled with lions and bears. The first creature to reach her was the lioness. It came running up to her, but rather than attack, the lioness turned and adopted a posture of protection at Thecla's feet.

A bear charged, but before it could reach Thecla, the lioness killed it. Next, a male lion attacked, but again the lioness fought to protect Thecla. The struggle ended with the death of both lions, their bodies locked in combat at her feet. The masters of the game whipped and goaded the remaining animals toward their prey. But beast after fierce beast cowered and refused to attack. The crowd fell silent, as the fear of the Lord hushed the noisy arena. Thecla lifted her voice and prayed boldly.

The governor stood to his feet and stopped the games. He demanded to know who this woman was and what was the source of this power she possessed. She answered, "I am the handmaid of the living God . . . I have believed on that Son in whom God is well pleased. For he alone is the way of salvation and the substance of life immortal . . . whosoever believeth not on him, shall not live . . ."

227

The governor commanded clothes to be brought to her and ordered her release. Hundreds if not thousands were converted to Christ that day, and the early church annals reported that the women of Antioch praised God with one voice until the city shook with the sound.

Thecla went on to live a long, full life and preached the gospel until she died in her nineties.

Living with Brash Boldness

What made this woman Thecla so powerful? She was naked and unashamed because at the revelation of Jesus she discovered herself. Even though she was a new convert, she made a compelling ambassador. As she raised her voice in prayer, she demonstrated courage in the face of death. A brave daughter who might be denied the right to preach fully clothed in many a pulpit won a multitude of converts naked and surrounded by beasts in a cruel coliseum. When I read stories like this, I like to think Eve smiles. (I am sure Sarah does too!) For the battle Eve lost in the intimate nurture and safety of a garden has been won many times over by reborn daughters in arenas of open hostility.

The crowd had gathered to see an execution, but instead they witnessed the reversal of the fall. May our lives continue this legacy. As we daily declare that our salvation and substance are found in Christ alone, we increase our capacity to be filled with him and hasten his return.

Today we know more about the Bible than at any other time in our human history. And yet where has this knowledge brought us? We have an abundance of information and a glaring lack of transformation. I fear in many ways and on many fronts intellect and talent have been substituted for God's Word and the guidance of his Holy Spirit.

I want more. What I sense in my spirit is an outpouring and harvest without rival.

This broken world needs to see God's power. Perhaps it is time we echo the prayers of the early church.

> So now, Lord, listen to their threats to harm us and empower us, as your servants, to speak the word of God freely and courageously. Stretch out your hand of power through us to heal, and to move in signs and wonders by the name of your holy Son, Jesus! (Acts 4:29–30 TPT)

And what did these prayers set in motion?

> At that moment the earth shook beneath them, causing the building they were in to tremble. Each one of them was filled with the Holy Spirit, and they proclaimed the word of God with unrestrained boldness. (Acts 4:31 TPT)

It is time for God's Word to be proclaimed with unhindered brash boldness. In many ways, the challenges Thecla faced were not that different from our own. There was outrage when she decided to take a path that was unexpected and to live a life that was consecrated. Family members tried to hold her back, the government tried to legislate her faith, men tried to take her by force and suppress what they saw as rebellion. And yet all along she was the one who was truly free. Whether she lived or died had no bearing on who she knew she was . . . she was a handmaiden of the Most High God.

A Life without Rival

We live in a day and age when everything around us is tempest tossed. If you know who you are and whose you are . . . you will stand. We have chosen a life without rival . . . a life that can only be constructed by the Holy Spirit.

> Since this is the kind of life we have chosen, the life of the Spirit, let us make sure that we *do not just hold it as an idea* in our heads or a sentiment in our hearts, but *work out its implications in every detail of our lives.* That means *we will not compare ourselves with each other* as if one of us were better and another worse. We have far more interesting things to do with our lives. *Each of us is an original.* (Gal. 5:25–26 Message)

And so we end where we began.

This unique expression of *you* as an original will lead to a life in keeping with the Spirit. You were not created for comparison . . . you were created for God's Son. Your heavenly Father wrote out the intimate details of your life in his book long before you drew your first breath. He wrote your life with living letters. No one else can live your story. It is time your pages came alive. Living the story lines written for others will leave what the Spirit has written of you unfulfilled. Each and every one of us has a specific course and destiny. The Holy Spirit's direction is essential if you are going to live a life without rival. This Spirit-led life is not merely a concept or a romantic hope—it is an expression

You were not created for comparison . . . you were created for God's Son.

of spiritual discipline and a personal act of worship. A life of devotion, not distraction. With each act of obedience in both your intimate and your public life, God will detail his purpose for your life and his voice to you will grow in clarity.

Your life and all of its potential is a God-given entrustment. It would be a shame if all that is in you were like so much treasure and talents buried under the opinions and expectations of strangers. You are not here on earth as a spectator. You have far more important and interesting things to do with your life. It is time you knew this.

Your future is now.

We have this point in time. None of us is promised tomorrow, but you know this moment is yours. And the power of your choices can redeem all your moments.

You have been seeded with a stunning story of promise. The book of your life can remain closed, or you can continue to turn the pages. Listen to Paul's message to the Galatians:

> Make a careful exploration of who you are and the work you have been given, and then sink yourself into that. Don't be impressed with yourself. Don't compare yourself with others. Each of you must take responsibility for doing the creative best you can with your own life. (Gal. 6:4–5 Message)

It is so hard to know who you are if you are too busy looking at who you are not or at who everyone else is. You must know *who you are* in this journey called life if you are to walk and not faint.

> Look carefully then how you walk, not as unwise but as wise, making the best use of the time, because the days are evil. (Eph. 5:15–16)

If you are not intentional with your time, your days will float away from you as you are pushed and pulled by demands and distractions. When you lay aside this book, pick up pen and paper. Sort through what are wise and unwise uses of your time. I need you to open up your days so you can dream again.

Carefully tie your goals to your dreams. So daughter without rival, what do you dream? You may counter that your life is boring or mundane. I didn't ask you for a status report. What is your passion? If you have lost it, get back into the presence of God until you find it again. Clear your head and your heart. Go for a walk, listen to worship music, and reconnect with the well of your soul.

You are never too old, never too poor, never too rich, never too educated, and never too uneducated to set goals or dream dreams. You are also never too young.

There are times when I look out upon the landscape of Christian women today and I am utterly stunned by so many who are doing this dance of life and ministry so very well. There are so many beautiful, brave, godly young women on the front lines right now that I find my heart so full of hope. I begin to wonder if I can move into less of a climb and more of a slide position. Recently, while pondering this very thing, I heard the Holy Spirit correct me. *Their coming up does not mean you step back. You must continue to forge ahead. I never meant them to push you aside; let them push you up.*

My trajectory of "up" may look different than it has, but I never hear God say look down, or drop your chin. He says lift it. When his daughters gather in unity, I see his glory.

So, lovely one, I will share with you my passion. You. I pray I will always labor that Christ the anointed One would be formed in you. I long to see you well equipped and positioned in him to find what was originally entrusted to you. I long to help you on your dearest quest, to know him. As I wrote this book, I realized I had tackled far too big of a subject, for we live in a day that is rife with rivals vying for our affection. Paul lived in a different day, and yet the church he loved faced similar struggles.

> For I feel a divine jealousy for you, since I betrothed you to one husband, to present you as a pure virgin to Christ. But I am afraid that as the serpent deceived Eve by his cunning, your thoughts will be led astray from a sincere and pure devotion to Christ. For if someone comes and proclaims another Jesus than the one we proclaimed, or if you receive a different spirit from the one you received, or if you accept a different gospel from the one you accepted, you put up with it readily enough. (2 Cor. 11:2–4)

Or as The Message translates this passage:

> The thing that has me so upset is that I care about you so much—this is the passion of God burning inside me! I promised your hand in marriage to Christ, presented you as a pure virgin to her husband. And now I'm afraid that exactly as the Snake seduced Eve with his smooth patter, you are being lured away from the simple purity of your love for Christ. It seems that if someone shows up preaching quite another Jesus than we preached—different spirit, different message—you put up with him quite nicely.

Hear me as a mother—nay, a grandmother: you were not made for the compromise of comparison. The Creator wove *his* originality into your DNA. Only you can give the unique expression of his love and glory, and the fruits and rewards of how you do this will travel with you into eternity.

Eternal Crowns

I began the book by unpacking who you are and who God is and seek to close it with what we have been given. In addition to the exceeding great and precious promises that position us to be partakers of God's divine nature, there is the adornment of authority.

I like jewelry, but not just any jewelry. I love jewelry with a story. My wedding rings represent the story of our marriage. I have rings that were given to me at the birth of each son. I have a necklace that's a sword, an arrow bracelet, and another that represents what it means to fight like a girl. I have pieces that are gifts from friends or that are tied to significant seasons or changes in my life. The meaning or timing behind the gift is how I determine if a piece of jewelry is an adornment or an accessory.

I love the story *Hinds' Feet on High Places* by Hannah Hurnard. It came into my life when I was in my midtwenties and has stayed with me ever since. I read it to my children when they were young, and I read it to myself whenever the need arises. In this allegory, a young woman filled with fears travels from her home to the high places where perfect love casts out fear. Along the way there are many twists, turns, and trials. At each place, the heroine, Much-Afraid, builds an altar and picks up a stone of remembrance that she carries with her in a pouch. At one point, she is so discouraged and the promise seems so far off that she is tempted to toss aside these memorial rocks as worthless reminders of her disappointment. On second thought she keeps them, which is a good thing, because later each stone is transformed into a jewel in her crown.

Scholars believe there are five specific crowns mentioned in Scripture.[2] There is the Crown of Righteousness, which we receive when we exchange our sin and shame for Christ's righteousness and he crowns us with his salvation. There is the Crown of Rejoicing; this one is reserved for those who worship and praise God regardless of their circumstances. Next is the Crown of Glory for those who long for his glorious reappearing. On these last few pages I want to highlight the remaining two.

The Imperishable Crown

The Imperishable Crown is the one spoken of in 1 Corinthians 9:24–27:

> Do you not know that in a race all the runners run, but only one receives the prize? So run that you may obtain it. Every athlete exercises self-control in all things. They do it to receive a perishable wreath, but we an imperishable. So I do not run aimlessly; I do not box as one beating the air. But I discipline my body and keep it under control, lest after preaching to others I myself should be disqualified.

This crown is won by racing, and the way we train affects the way we run. Training is not fun, but neither is being disqualified or losing a race. In so many ways the Holy Spirit is our trainer.

> Don't grieve God. Don't break his heart. His Holy Spirit, moving and breathing in you, is the most intimate part of

your life, making you fit for himself. Don't take such a gift for granted. (Eph. 4:30 Message)

All things are lawful, but not all things contribute to godliness and a well-run race. God knows what it will take. He knows when we need to speed up or slow down. He knows whom we should train with and whom we need to stay away from. We are the ones who benefit when we follow his instructions. We are not competing for the perishable; we are racing toward eternity.

> Do not lay up for yourselves treasures on earth, where moth and rust destroy and where thieves break in and steal, but lay up for yourselves treasures in heaven, where neither moth nor rust destroys and where thieves do not break in and steal. For where your treasure is, there your heart will be also. (Matt. 6:19–21)

When your heart is in heaven, you will find your way there. As we have already explored, this treasure is carried in your heart and its guardian is love. We live in a world pregnant with words, ideas, books, thoughts, social connections, beauty, creativity, and wisdom. So much of it is wonderful. But there is a dangerous pull from this world that would try to weigh you down so you cannot run your race. We are warned:

> Do not love the world or the things in the world. If anyone loves the world, the love of the Father is not in him. For all that is in the world—the desires of the flesh and the desires of the eyes and pride of life—is not from the Father but is from the world. And the world is passing away along with its desires, but whoever does the will of God abides forever. (1 John 2:15–17)

These are the things that bind and tether us by their attachment to the ways of earth.

The passions of the world break down into three categories:

1. The desires of the flesh or wanting your own way.
2. The desires of the eyes or wanting everything you see.
3. The pride of life or wanting to appear important.

Each of us will wrestle with at least one of these rivals if not all three at different stages in our lives. There are countless ways these can play out in your life, and each of these driving desires can look different in changing seasons. When we were first married and without children, I was very selfish. I think it would be fair to say I wanted my own way and I wanted a lot that I saw. Thankfully, we didn't have the money to support my bad behavior, but that didn't mean I didn't see things and want them anyway. Then I had three kids in five years, and all I wanted was a nap! As for wanting to appear important, as I get older I am more than content to be important to my family, friends, and the handful of daughters who have come my way.

These driving passions are attached to a world that is destined to crumble under the weight of eternity. Everything from social media to music, commercials, and entertainment tends to feed these desires. Never in the history of humans have we had such intimate access to people with whom we have no relationship. When people have a hard time connecting with the people they can see (their friends and families), it is not surprising that connecting with a God they cannot see would pose a challenge.

But whoever does the will of God abides forever. (1 John 2:17)

To detach from this world, we lay down our will and embrace God's. In him we find the cure for these dangerous attachments.

> You must love the Lord God with all your heart, all your passion, all your energy, and your every thought. And you must love your neighbor as well as you love yourself. (Luke 10:27 TPT)

When the love of God abounds in your life, this earth's pull lessens. As I meditate on God and let him love me, I find that I am easier on myself. When I am easier on myself, I am more loving to others. When I am God focused and loving, then I am much less likely to pursue empty things, because my relationships fill in the gap.

> Do you not know that friendship with the world is enmity with God? Therefore whoever wishes to be a friend of the world makes himself an enemy of God. (James 4:4)

I sometimes wonder if we take this Scripture seriously or imagine that it no longer applies in our dispensation of grace. It is hard to imagine anyone ever knowingly choosing to set themselves in opposition to their Creator. Paul dealt with an adulterous people who wanted to live under both the law and grace, and James is addressing those who have an eternal covenant but who like Lot's wife struggle with a worldly attachment.

Notice this drift begins with but a wish or a desire to befriend the world. What exactly is James addressing here? Having friends in this world or even friends who are worldly is not the same thing as befriending the world. We are to be a friend *to* the world but not friends *with* the world. The first describes how we relate to the world's inhabitants; the second is friendship with its system. You will never have authority over what you are under the sway of. We are called to acts of compassion for our world rather than to sympathy with it. This means:

We clothe the naked in the world, rather than get naked with the world.

Feed the hungry in the world rather than hunger for the world.

We are agents of healing who have been called to the bedside of a hurting world, not to be in bed with the world.

Even with individuals we relate to them as ambassadors of another kingdom where our King's commands are honored. This means the day will come when this relationship will be challenged.

To win this crown, we must abandon our rivalry with fear and embrace God's call to love him, others, and ourselves.

The Crown of Life

And then there is the last crown . . . the Crown of Life. By all accounts this could also be called the martyr's crown. Many of the heroes listed in the book of Hebrews' "Hall of Faith" found this crown as did Stephen, Peter, and so very many followers of Christ whom we will never know the name of this side of eternity. There are those who *give all*. This crown is purchased at a cost without rival.

> Be faithful unto death, and I will give you the crown of life. He who has an ear, let him hear what the Spirit says to the churches. The one who conquers will not be hurt by the second death. (Rev. 2:10–11)

I love how The Message states verse 10: "I have a Life-Crown sized and ready for you."

We live in a day and age when more and more hearts will fail from fear. Violence, disease, famine, and war breed the fear of death. Slander, accusation, and persecution breed the fear of man. It is so obvious that Satan wants to overwhelm us all into inaction or push us into reaction. Like Nero, Satan wants to stun us with cruelty and horror on one side and seduce us with riches and lust on the other. More than anything our enemy would like us to stay by the wishing wells, fretting and tossing coins. But we need depth to win this crown.

We need depth to win this crown.

Recently, three horrific stories found their way to me in the span of one day. Two of them came via links from one of my spiritual daughters. She and her family head up an organization committed to fighting sex trafficking in Israel. In the first link, I read of the tragic suicide of 150 young girls and women who had been captured by ISIS and held as sex slaves. As though any insult needed to be added to this grievous injury, their captors fed their bodies to the dogs. In disbelief I read the account multiple times. Can evil this blatant truly exist? Even as I now type these words, I see a fleeting image of dogs viciously tearing these girls' bodies apart. As I flinch in horror at the image in my mind's eye, the words of Revelation 12:17 return to me:

> Then the dragon became furious with the woman and went off to make war on the rest of her offspring, on those who keep the commandments of God and hold to the testimony of Jesus.

This type of thing is far too cruel for humans . . . it is dragon rage.

This fury is pointed at "the Woman" and at "the children who keep God's commands and hold firm to the witness of Jesus" (Rev. 12:17 Message). Over the last decade I have seen this dark image increase in evil and reach to unimaginable proportions.

The next link I opened spoke of awarding sex slaves as prizes to men who had memorized the Qur'an. There was also a reference to the rape of infidels as acts of worship. Sadly, I fear that by the time this book goes to print many more horrific waves of atrocities will have buried these stories in their wake.

The third one came directly to me through a staff email. We have a key man who works with us to coordinate the distribution of free resources in countries where persecution or poverty limits people's access to Christian resources. One of our brave friends in the Middle East had been killed in a shelling directed at Christians in Syria. In the course of explaining the circumstance of this man's death, our contact wrote, "Some are called to give much, others give all."

I was stunned. As I drove to an appointment, I tried to mentally compose a letter to his widow. I felt that anything I said would be an insult to his life and her circumstances. *Sorry* seemed shallow, *thank you* seemed wrong. I would write her a note from the safety of a home that has never known the death of a martyr. I have worship music at my fingertips and more books and Bibles than I can read. My pantry is filled with food, my closet with clothes, and tonight when I babysit my grandchildren, they will laugh and play, oblivious that this type of pain exists in the lives of our brothers and sisters.

I felt ashamed. I suddenly felt as though my life was an insulated, empty shell and everything I knew and had was as fragile as the bubbles my grandchildren blow. I wanted to call someone. A woman who was older and wiser . . . who would simply understand what I was going through even if she could not answer the questions raging within me.

I had so many "whys." Why do I have so much when women across the ocean were so desperate they would rather take their lives than live another moment? Where was the justice? I wanted to process the disparity of the anguish I felt. Then I realized I was comparing. I was right to feel the contrast, but comparison was useless. There was no answer. There is only a serpent that has become a dragon. Under the influence of dragons men and women do awful things to one another. I realized I had a choice. I could keep asking angry questions, or I could allow the question marks in my life to be changed to exclamation marks. I wiped my tears and decided that their lives would serve to punctuate mine.

These stories of persecution aren't new—they come in every age. At fifty-five I must mature into a woman who doesn't wrestle with questions I can never answer this side of eternity. Age alone cannot make sense out of the senseless. We are on a fast track, and the events of our day serve to make eternity that much more attractive. Which is all the more reason to labor well while we can. Only in eternity will the story make sense, but here and now we can pray and know we are heard when our hearts are free from competition, jealousy, and comparisons.

> You were all called to travel on the same road and in the same direction, so stay together, both outwardly and inwardly. You

have one Master, one faith, one baptism, one God and Father of all, who rules over all, works through all, and is present in all. Everything you are and think and do is permeated with Oneness. But that doesn't mean you should all look and speak and act the same. Out of the generosity of Christ, each of us is given his own gift. (Eph. 4:4–7 Message)

Live Your Life!

So much has been given to us. Our unique perspective is a gift. What we have seen and experienced is a gift. We have a choice. We can let it overwhelm us and do nothing. We can treat it as common and allow it to underwhelm us. Or we can live in a case of constant wonder. Pondering the power of our moment, then moving forward.

Over the last decade I have written of lioness women and girls with swords and crosses, of fighting like a girl and kisses that make girls cry rather than nurture their soul. And now I write in the hope that all that waits within you is realized. Because

You, daughter, are called to a life without rival.
Loved by a Father without rival.
Alive in a time without rival.
Hailing from a nation without rival.
Serving a God without rival.
Bought by a sacrifice without rival.
Entrusted with a name without rival.
Empowered by his Spirit without rival.
Versed in a language without rival.

Part of a body without rival.

Given a commission without rival.

Equipped with a weapon without rival.

Engaged in a war without rival.

Called to prayers without rival.

Before us are opportunities without rival, for we are

Positioned for a harvest without rival and

Destined for an eternity without rival . . .

Let us now live a life that is unrivaled in beauty, power, virtue, and reach . . . some giving much, others giving all.

Stand before God, radiant in hope, faithful in serving, and loving in all you do. For you, my friend and sister, have a destiny without rival. Now go with the courage born of love and boldly—brashly—live it.

Discussion Questions

1. What did the story of Thecla speak to you?
2. Describe the difference between friendship with the world and being a friend to the world.
3. What are the areas in your life where you need to change the punctuation?
4. What is the next step you will take toward your life without rival?

Discussion Questions

I f you're reading this book as part of the *Insights to a Life without Rival* study (which is a really great idea!), I recommend that you watch each week's video session and unpack the corresponding discussion questions as a group. The video sessions will parallel and amplify major themes from this book, so it's ideal for all participants to both watch the sessions and read the book during the six-week study.

Enjoy!

Week 1

This week corresponds with video session 1: Love Fearlessly
Week 1 highlights themes found in chapters 1 and 7.

1. What are the areas of life where you find it difficult to love fearlessly?
2. What undermines and attacks your identity?
3. What are a few of the unique things about you? How can you celebrate and develop these?

Week 2

This week corresponds with video session 2: Don't Settle for Crumbs and Rumors

Week 2 highlights themes found in chapter 2.

1. What is an area in your relationship with God that feels more like crumbs and leftovers than a banquet?
2. Whom does God whisper that you truly are?
3. What portion of the I AM do you need to embrace?

Week 3

This week corresponds with video session 3: Be Part of the Conversation

Week 3 highlights themes found in chapter 3.

1. What are some of the conversations you need to be a part of?
2. Where have you mistaken silence for submission?
3. What are you hiding from?
4. What promise (or promises) are you laughing at and lying about?

Week 4

This week corresponds with video session 4: Live Uniquely

Week 4 highlights themes found in chapters 4 and 5.

1. Have you allowed yourself to be labeled or pigeonholed? If so, what steps can you take to move away from these labels?

2. In what areas have you allowed comparison to rob you of your joy?

3. In what ways can you change your response to a rival and increase your "grit factor"?

Week 5

This week corresponds with video session 5: Leave a Redemptive Legacy

Week 5 highlights themes found in chapter 6.

1. Have you ever allowed people to call you back when God had called you out? How can you change that?

2. Have you ever experienced gender prejudice? Where did this happen?

3. What is your hope for the daughters?

Week 6

This week corresponds with video session 6: Pursue the Eternal Story

Week 6 highlights themes found in chapter 10.

1. What does it mean to be part of an eternal story? How does comparison undermine this?

2. How do you see our days: frightening or exciting? Why do you have this outlook?

3. Are there areas where you need to be more of a friend to the world and less of a friend of its system? What are some steps you could take to see this happen?

4. What are some of the ways you can go all in?

Notes

Chapter 3: A Promise without Rival

1. Though the true meaning of *selah* is not known, many think it is a liturgical notation. The Amplified Bible translates *selah* as "pause, and think of that."

Chapter 5: When You're Seen as a Rival

1. A. L. Duckworth, C. Peterson, M. D. Matthews, and D. R. Kelly, "Grit: Perseverance and Passion for Long-Term Goals," *Journal of Personality and Social Psychology* 92, no. 6 (2007): 1087.

2. Malcom Gladwell, *David and Goliath: Underdogs, Misfits, and the Art of Battling Giants* (New York: Little, Brown and Co., 2013).

Chapter 6: Gender without Rival

1. Mark Driscoll, *On Church Leadership* (Wheaton, IL: Crossway, 2008).

2. Ibid.

3. Kris Vallotton, *Fashioned to Reign* (Grand Rapids: Chosen, 2013), chap. 7.

4. Gilbert Bilezikian, *Beyond Sex Roles: What the Bible Says about a Woman's Place in Church and Family*, 3rd ed. (Grand Rapids: Baker, 2006).

Chapter 7: The Rivalry of Fear and Love

1. C. S. Lewis, *The Four Loves* (New York: Harcourt Brace Jovanovich, 1960).

2. Kent M. Keith, *The Paradoxical Commandments* (Makawao, HI: Inner Ocean, 2001).

Chapter 9: A Daughter without Rival

1. http://oca.org/saints/lives/2015/05/10/39-sunday-of-the-samaritan-woman.

2. http://www.pravoslavie.ru/english/print79178.htm.

3. Christopher Henry Dawson, *Religion and World History: A Selection from the Works of Christopher Dawson* (Garden City, NJ: Image Books, 1975).

4. The facts reported in this paragraph are culled from the following accounts: Robyn Dixon, "At Kenya College, Christian Students Foretold Massacre," *Los Angeles Times*, April 5, 2015; "Gunmen Kill 147 at University in Kenya," *Chicago Tribune*, April 3, 2015; "At Least 147 Killed in Islamic Terror Attack at Kenya University Targeting Christian Students," *KTLA.com*, April 2, 2015.

Chapter 10: A Life Unrivaled

1. For more on the life of Thecla, see these sources: http://www.pbs.org/wgbh/pages/frontline/shows/religion/maps/primary/thecla.html (the account from the Apocryphal Acts); http://www.antiochian.org/life_of_thekla; http://dce.oca.org/assets/templates/bulletin.cfm?mode=html&id=101; http://www.newadvent.org/cathen/14564a.htm.

2. Henry Clarence Thiessen, *Lectures in Systematic Theology* (Grand Rapids: Eerdmans, 1979), 389.

Lisa Bevere is a sought-after international speaker, a bestselling author, and the cohost of *The Messenger* television program, which is broadcast in more than two hundred countries. The author of *Lioness Arising*, *Girls with Swords*, and *Fight Like a Girl*, Lisa is a frequent guest on *Life Today* and has been a speaker at Women of Faith, Joyce Meyer conferences, and Hillsong Church. She and her husband, John, have four sons and live in Colorado. Learn more at www.lisabevere.com.

WITHOUT
RIVAL

STAY ENGAGED
with *Without Rival* and Lisa Bevere

#WithoutRival

LisaBevere.com

What would it look like to live free from comparison and embrace the unique story God is telling through your life?

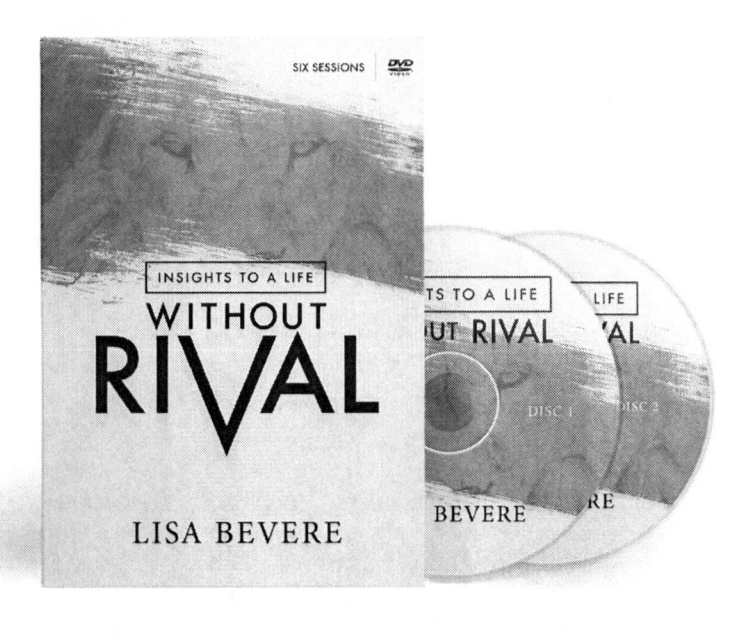

In *Insights to a Life without Rival*, Lisa Bevere invites you on a journey to discover this life beyond compare.

Includes
6 video sessions on 2 DVDs *(18 min. each)*

Order Today
MessengerInternational.org/store
Call: 1-800-648-1477

Pastors and leaders, connect with Messenger International's Church Relations team to receive a special resource discount!

BOOKS BY LISA

Be Angry but Don't Blow It!
Fight Like a Girl*
Girls with Swords*
It's Not How You Look, It's What You See
Kissed the Girls and Made Them Cry*

Lioness Arising*
Nurture*
Out of Control and Loving It!
The True Measure of a Woman
You Are Not What You Weigh

*Available in curriculum format

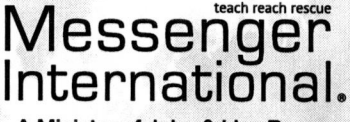

teach reach rescue
Messenger
International.
A Ministry of John & Lisa Bevere

Messenger International was founded by John and Lisa Bevere in 1990. In over two decades of ministry, Messenger International's God-entrusted messages have transformed millions of lives worldwide. Today, our mission to teach, reach, and rescue encompasses a wide variety of efforts to disciple the nations.

Call: 1-800-648-1477

Email: Mail@MessengerInternational.org

Visit us online at: MessengerInternational.org

Connect with Lisa Bevere

LisaBevere.com